DR BERNIE WADE

WAR ON EARTH

SATAN'S PLAN TO ENSLAVE MANKIND

War on Earth
Satan's Plan to Enslave Mankind
Copyright © 2022 Bernie L. Wade

All rights reserved. No part of this publication may be reproduced, distributed or transmitted in any form or by any means, without prior written permission. Unless otherwise identified, scripture quotations are from the King James Version of the Bible.

Publisher
Dreamer Reign, LLC
P.O. Box 291354
Port Orange, FL 32129

www.dreamerreign.com

For Worldwide Distribution
Printed in the U.S.A.

ISBN: 9781952253171
Library of Congress Control Number: 2022914275

Cover Design: C Marcel Wiggins

CONTENTS

DEDICATION 4
FOREWORD 5
PREFACE 6
CHAPTER ONE – In the beginning 17
    The message is uncomplicated 20
    The challenge 23
    Legacy 25
CHAPTER TWO – War on mankind 31
    Eden: The garden of God 35
    Planning the deception 39
CHAPTER THREE – Theophany and Christophany 43
    Angel of the Lord 45
    Melchizedek 47
    Michael the Archangel 48
CHAPTER FOUR – Who is satan? 53
    The serpent 58
    Deceiver 62
    Lucifer 76
CHAPTER FIVE – Two trees in the garden 97
    The tree of life 104
CHAPTER SIX – Angels 111
CHAPTER SEVEN – Set the trumpet to your mouth 129
CHAPTER EIGHT – Satan is defeated 143
    War in Heaven 152
    The woman gives birth to a child 156
    The woman persecuted 162

DEDICATION

To my wife, Daisy, who took a chance on us making it through life together. Nearly 40 years later, it seems to be working!

To my mother, Georgia Ann (Gillespie) Wade, who said, "the measure of great men is how they treat others." Mom, I'm still working on it.

FOREWORD

I have known Bishop Bernie Wade and his family for many years. I consider him a dear and close friend and a co-laborer in God's Kingdom. He is a true Holy Spirit filled—present day Historian. I always find our conversations enlightening and insightful.

"War on Earth" is masterfully thought out and written. He answers many of the age old questions that have been in the back of folks minds, minister's, and saint's for decades. Some, because of ignorance, (simply a lack of information) or fearful of "rocking the boat," have stayed away from or at best, skirted the issues.

Bishop Bernie Wade unveils God's original purpose and intent for man, thus culminating in the salvation and redemption of humanity after Adam's fall. The truths revealed and released in the chapters and pages to follow, will challenge the seasoned saints, while shedding tremendous light and insight to the new believer.

This book will open the door of illumination to a desperately lethargic and complacent church; mankind doesn't have to remain in the dark any longer. You will be challenged and strengthened as you embark on what you are about to read.

—Dr. Don Hughes

PREFACE

"I would rather be what God chose to make me than the most glorious creature that I could think of; for to have been thought about, born in God's thought, and then made by God, is the dearest, grandest and most precious thing in all thinking." —George MacDonald

The Book of Genesis derives its name from the opening stanza, "In the beginning…" Genesis is the book of the beginning for all mankind and all the creatures that inhabit this planet. Genesis is unique as there is no other book that chronicles the beginning of mankind from the perspective of God. Right after this stanza is the word "God." "In the beginning God…" In other words, every beginning starts with God. He should be first in everything we do, think, plan, and more.[1]

In this unpretentious phrase, we also learn that everything has a beginning — even the earth. Apostle John said it more profoundly, "In the beginning was the Word!"[2] This lets us know that God was indeed at the beginning! Before there was a creation narrative in Genesis chapter two, God was alone, standing on nothing.[3]

From Apostle John, we also learn that even the Word was a part of God. Thus, when Moses wrote about creation, he saw the Word in action. Furthermore, Apostle John tells us that the Word (God) became flesh (Jesus Christ)! John's emphasis is on the

---
1   Acts 17:28
2   John 1:1
3   Hebrews Chapter 6

incarnation's effect on the human quest for the vision of God. He says that in this life we have not been able to see God with our normal human sight — until now. Jesus claims, "Anyone who has seen Me has seen the Father."[4]

The incarnation has brought a new way to apprehend God. Yet, even now it is not God in His essence that is seen,[5] for creatures do not have the capacity to apprehend God in Himself. We can only see Him as He makes Himself accessible to our limited organs of perception.[6] Furthermore, the opponents saw Jesus but did not recognize His deity, so the other two forms of sight are also required. Thus, the incarnation adds to the complexity of Scripture on this subject, but it also provides the criterion for assessing claims to have seen God. Throughout this Gospel, John will deny such claims made by Jewish mystics.[7]

Theologians debate if the phrase "in the beginning" is speaking about the beginning of everything or the beginning for mankind. Whether or not it is about the beginning of everything, it is certainly the beginning for mankind. It is apparent the entire Bible was written to mankind and for mankind. *"All Scripture is God-breathed and is useful for teaching, rebuking, correcting and training in righteousness, so that the servant of God may be thoroughly equipped for every good work."*[8]

---

4 John 14:9
5 cf. 1 Tim 6:16
6 cf. Chrysostom In John 15.1
7 cf. 1:51; 3:13; 6:46; 14:8-9
8 2 Timothy 3:16-17

There is considerable debate among scientists and theologians as to whether or not the Universe had a physical beginning. Some expect that the Universe was always here. These experts have conceived many theories, but all of them are flawed by the reasoning of man. For centuries the general belief by scientists was that the earth was without beginning and therefore always existed. That changed when Einstein, Hubble, and others confirmed that the Universe has a beginning.[9]

The concept that the earth had a beginning gave credence to the creation narrative and creation scientists. If the earth has a beginning, it certainly could have a creator. In response to creation science, Georges Lemaître, who was both a Catholic priest and a scientist, offered the Big Bang Theory with all its flaws.[10]

We can be positive that in giving Moses the details that became the book of Genesis, God was giving mankind information that the Universe has a beginning. Firstly, the information was to inform the children of Israel and by extension all of mankind. Just like a father explaining to his children about things that happened when they were too young to remember or before they were born, God makes it clear that He alone created the Universe in which mankind lives.[11]

How much time was there before God created the earth —

---

9   sciencedaily.com/releases/2014/02/140217102545.htm

10   Cosmic Horizons: Astronomy at the Cutting. Steven Soter. Neil deGrasse Tyson. New Press. © 2000

11   see e.g. 1 Chronicles 29:14–16, Acts 17:24–28, and Romans 11:33–36

we are not informed. So, we may speculate any amount of time we like. The Roman cleric Augustine contended that there was no time before Genesis chapter one verse one.[12] His expectation is that Moses captured the entire story of God and all creation in a couple of chapters. Even if it is true that "In the beginning" is intended to mean at the very beginning of time, we know that before all of that there was God. Time was created by God for man.[13] Genesis chapter one certainly does not explain the beginning of God. Theophilus[14] writes of God: "The form of God is ineffable...in glory uncontainable, in well doing indescribable...He is without beginning because He is uncreated, and He is unchangeable because He is immortal."[15]

Augustine makes many assumptions that have become generally accepted by theologians. It may well be that Augustine's assumptions helped some of his former associates among the Manicheans,[16] but for those were filled with the Holy Ghost his assumptions seem to present as pagan or as Apostle Paul said, "another gospel."

Some of his ideas might present as good notions but are very flawed.[17] To follow Augustine's theory, God, who is not in time,

---

12   The Literal Meaning of Genesis, John Hammond Taylor, Newman Pres, 1982.
13   Genesis 1:1; Exodus 20:8–11; Ecclesiastes 11:5; John 1:3; Colossians 1:16–17
14   https://en.wikipedia.org/wiki/Theophilus_(biblical)
15   ad Autol. 1.3
16   britannica.com/topic/Manichaeism
17   On the literal interpretation of Genesis, an unfinished book / by Augustine, Saint, Bishop of Hippo. Published 1990. Call Number: BR61 .F38 v. 84 1991

created the Universe at the very second He came into being. This is difficult to understand let alone explain and is mere conjecture on Augustine's part. Holes and gaps in Scripture are equally hard to imagine. Unfortunately, men have presented a plethora of dogmas and inserted them into the book of Genesis. Among the many rationales offered by theologians is that Genesis chapter one was the beginning of everything. For example: Augustine amalgamated the creation of angels as happening somewhere in the creation narrative even though there is no mention of angels. If God created angels during that time period, certainly it would be relevant to the presentation of the topic. However, if angels were created beforehand as they obviously were then it would be irrelevant to the topic presented in Genesis. God made everything we have no doubt. Fortunately, we do not need the help of mankind's hypothesis if we just trust God to be our source of information.

The Bible is the story about God and mankind.[18] There may be some book somewhere in the eons of time where God tells the angels about their genesis, but that would not be in this realm. Such a book (if it exists) would have little or no bearing on mankind.

How long before Genesis chapter one, verse one did God create angels is not important? It is evident that God created them and they were one of many building stones in God's creation plan. The reason we say building stones is because God was continuing to improve His creation and would improve on the same until the creation of Adam and Eve when He was pleased with His creation

---

Located: Falvey West - Ground Floor

18 2 Peter 1:20-21

and called it very good![19]

> *"You are the Lord, you alone; you have made Heaven, the Heaven of Heavens, with all their host...and the host of Heaven worships you."*[20]

The creation of angels appears to have been before the events recorded here on Earth by Moses. Moses makes no attempt to exclude that there may be activity preceding what God gave him. Rather, Moses as the leader of the children of Israel, is focused on the events that are relevant to his mission. Scripture records that the angels celebrated God's creation. In response to Augustine's explanation, God might well ask Augustine, "Where were you when I laid the earth's foundation ...and all the angels shouted for joy?"[21]

"The time of the creation of angels is something that the Bible does not specifically mention. Angelic existence dates back before the creation of humans. How far back no one knows. They seem to have been in existence when the earth was created. Scripture indicates the angels shouted at God's creation of the earth—possibly before any material thing was made. They were definitely created before humanity. Beyond this, there is not enough information to be more specific."[22] About angels, the author of Hebrews designates that all angels are "spirits."[23] When Jesus appears to the disciples, He

---

19   Genesis 1:31
20   Nehemiah 9:6
21   Job 38:4,7
22   https://www.blueletterbible.org/faq/don_stewart/don_stewart_6.cfm
23   Hebrews 1:13-14

asserts that "spirits" don't have bodies like He does.[24]

In the Bible, angels cannot be seen by humans unless God reveals them.[25] However, as permitted by God, from time-to-time angels manifested and appeared to various people in Scripture.[26] Angels were created by God and inhabit a different realm. It seems unreasonable to expect that angels were not already created at the time of the Genesis account. We hold this point because there is no reference of angels in the creation story. It could be argued that there is no reference to their creation after the creation story either, except at the end of the creation narrative, which tells us that God ceased creating. This lends further credence to the point that they were created some time previously. Their exclusion from the Genesis narrative indicates their irrelevance to the general subject matter of creation and expands upon the point of God's monarchy.

"Thus says the Lord, the King of Israel, and his Redeemer, the Lord of hosts: 'I am the First and I am the Last; Besides Me there is no God.'"[27]

While God did not need a plethora of days to plan, organize, gather, and build His creation, man needed time to record the events. It is unmistakable that God's purpose in having Moses take several days[28] to write the narrative holds at least two functions:

---

24 Luke 24:39
25 Numbers 22:31, 2 Kings 6:17, Luke 2:13
26 Matthew 28:5; Hebrews 13:2
27 Isaiah 44:6-8.
28 Genesis Chapter 1.

First, the Genesis narrative takes what is likely a millisecond in the mind of God, but breaks it down (or unpacks it) so that we mortals can understand what happened. The point is so important that the Apostle John takes up the same theme, "In the beginning was the Word..."[29] It was important that this be communicated to mankind so we would have information about the pitfalls and the triumphs of those early days of antiquity. This is helpful so that we have the proper pattern to follow. That is the pattern God expected of those who were His faithful followers. There is more in the Genesis account than we realize. God created time for man. God, who is not bound by time, used this method to present things from eternity to mankind, who is in time.[30]

Secondly, the seven days Moses took record the narrative became pattern for the Sabbath day which God required of the children of Israel. Order and pattern are important to God. The Sabbath cycle represents more than just days. The Sabbath also represented years. The Sabbath also represented years.[31] The Sabbath was more than just about the people. God used the Sabbath to protect the land.[32] In establishing Himself as the God of the children of Israel, God wants to be certain they understand His bona fides.

The beginning of this writing came from research for a different writing project. During my research I began to wonder, "When did the war in Heaven mentioned in the book of Revelation

---

29 The Gospel of John 1:1
30 The Acts of the Apostles 1:7
31 Leviticus 25:8-11.
32 Leviticus 25:8-11.

begin?" It seems like it should be an easy answer. Theologians have generally said that this is a reference to Satan's original fall and occurs sometime before Genesis chapter three. This has been presented with little or no descent. Yet, careful analysis of the book of Genesis produces scriptural references for their theories. These venture that because of the events in chapter three of Genesis this "War in Heaven" by default must have occurred previously and so must be part of the creation story. Some contend it happened even before Genesis 1:1. No offense intended, but this seems like passages in the Bible when all the various kings' advisors presented themselves as being in agreement,[33] yet, they are not hearing from God. We need not accept conjecture in the place of Scripture God did not leave us without answers. He gave us His Word. In this writing, we will examine His Word. My research prompted other questions:

- What was Satan's sin? Satan's sin could not have merely been a violation recognized by the "thought police." His violation had to be profoundly serious since his actions provoked serious eternal consequences. It is obvious that his actions started a war with mankind.

- Where is the evidence of a sin that would have prompted or started a war that raged from before Genesis chapter three all the way to the book of Revelation?

- When did Satan commit this sin that theologians present as causing his (and his angel co-conspirators) expulsion from the Heavens?

---
33   https://en.wikipedia.org/wiki/Micaiah

- Why did Satan deceive Eve? Was he angry? Drunk? Insane?

- Why did Satan not attempt to deceive Adam? We have no indication that Satan even spoke to Adam.

- Why did God allow Satan to cause all the chaos in the Garden of Eden?

- Why did God not just pre-empt Satan's antics?

- Did God purposely allow Satan to tempt Eve as some teach?

- Why did Adam join in Satan's deception?

When I looked at what others had written on this subject, I found what was written to be less than satisfactory. The purpose of this writing is to point to the evidence that gives us answers to these questions. These answers are found in the text of Scripture that we already accept as inspired by the Holy Spirit. No need to draw information from unverifiable or pseudo sources. We do not need help from other sources; the 66 books we have provide amply. It is my expectation that what I have written on this subject will help you on your spiritual journey. Not only making you a better disciple of Jesus Christ, but also helping you help others to make the decision to live for Jesus!

Chapter 1
In the beginning

"My little children, these things write I unto you, that ye sin not. And if any man sin, we have an advocate with the Father, Jesus Christ the righteous: And he is the propitiation for our sins: and not for ours only, but also for the sins of the whole world. And hereby we do know that we know him, if we keep his commandments." [1]

In the Genesis account we learn many things about the origin of our Universe and the inhabitants of our planet. God is in eternity, not in time. Time was created by God so that mankind could better grasp God's vastness. We would say God unpacked the creation story so Moses could explain it in a manner that mankind could understand. From Genesis we grasp that God does not do things in some haphazard comportment or leave them to chance as some teach. "God's creation of time is another indication of His orderliness. God exists outside of time[2] as we know it, but He created

---

1   1 John 2:1-3
2   Hebrews 6:5, 9:26

time as a way for earth to mark changes. Time is orderly, sequential, and does not vary based on anything mankind can control. Time keeps us orderly. Rich or poor, young or old, we all have the same number of hours in a day. The sun will rise and set on schedule no matter what may be happening on earth. Because God is a God of order, He keeps everything in motion as He first designed. It is His orderly hand that holds the world in place."[3]

"It is in the Garden where we form the primary assumptions that influence our worship, lifestyle and our worldview. The balance of all future labor, scholarship, and testimony hinge upon the conclusions formed from the drama that unfolds in the first three chapters of Genesis."[4] The fall of mankind from immortality renders time more relevant. Time is irrelevant to immortal beings. Mortals mark everything by time.

The book of Genesis gives us proof that God has not left His creation to natural selection as Evolutionists like Anaximander of Miletus or Charles Darwin proposed.[5] Rather, God is the architect of the intelligence behind the design of all the patterns and order of the Universe. If there are indeed multiple universes as Hugh Everett[6] imagines, then God is the originator of them as well.

Some mortals seek to make the case that there is no God.

---

[3] https://www.gotquestions.org/God-of-order.html Hebrews 1:3; Colossians 1:17

[4] The Death of Adam. Frank Febus. Pg. 1

[5] https://www.nationalgeographic.org

[6] https://en.wikipedia.org/wiki/Many-worlds_interpretation

CHAPTER ONE: IN THE BEGINNING

Mankind in a fallen state is subject to many delusions. Projecting that there is no realm of immortality from which we are all fallen is one of those delusions. Those who imagine that there is no God are aptly addressed in Scripture.[7] Those who make-believe they can dodge the imprimatur of the Holy Spirit only deceive themselves.[8]

Consider the original audience for the information in the book of Genesis. God divinely gave the content to Moses on condition that Moses present it to the children of Israel. These were not modern people with laptop computers, mobile phones equipped with word processors, etc. These were not even people who were equipped with ink and paper. In other words, individually they were not equipped to keep this written down in some method. No, the important information in the book of Genesis, the other books of Moses, and all of Scripture are intended to be understood in the simplest manner possible. This is much like communicating with elementary age children. Not to say that the children of Israel were simple. To the contrary, they were well versed in many things. Perhaps these sons of God even better understood the practical application of what God was communicating in the creation narrative than we can from our more distant perspective. The writings that make up the Holy Scripture are not intended as some secret code or mystical book.

> *"The book of Genesis gives us proof that God has not left His creation to natural selection as Evolutionists like Anaximander of Miletus or Charles Darwin proposed. Rather, God is the architect of the intelligence behind the design of all the patterns and order of*

---
7   Psalm 14
8   Jeremiah 23:24

The Message Is Uncomplicated

God did not present a message to His people that they could not understand. What would be the point? No. The message He gave has a clear note, a certain sound![9] "Hear the word of the Lord from Deuteronomy 30:14 — *"The word of life is near to you..."*[10] "Here in Deuteronomy, Moses stands before God's people, exhaling a deep breath at the end of three mammoth sermons. No doubt the people are left suffering from sermon overload. Notice how Moses finishes his sermons in a climax that contains four points in 30:11-14.

The word of life is:
- Not too difficult.
- Not beyond your reach.
- Not up in Heaven.
- Not beyond the sea.

God is saying His Word is not too complicated for you. It's not inaccessible, it's not impractical, it's not impossible to understand, it's not only for the elite buffoons, and it's not just for your priest or pastor. You don't have to be some sort of spiritual superhuman to know God and to understand His Word. The meaning of His Word is not hidden to the majority, only to be discovered by the super clever or those who read hundreds of books. Moses says in 30:14, "The word is very near you." That statement is as simple as it is brief. God's Word is clear because He has brought it really near. Near enough to see, near enough to hear, near enough to touch, near

---

[9] 1 Corinthians 14:8.
[10] Deuteronomy 30:14

enough to know. "It's in your mouth and in your heart."[11] In the Book of Genesis Moses helps us understand these patterns:

- In the beginning - God started creation.

- The first day - light was created.

- The second day - the sky was created.

- The third day - dry land, seas, plants, and trees were created.

- The fourth day - the sun, moon and stars were created.

- The fifth day - creatures that live in the sea and creatures that fly were created.

- The sixth day - animals that live on the land and finally humans, made in the image of God were created.

- By day seven - God finished His work of creation and rested, making the seventh day a special holy day.

"So, are the days of Genesis 1 meant to be understood as regular 24-hour days? Yes and no. The seven-day week is meant to be understood as a regular human work week. But it does not automatically follow that Genesis 1 is revealing scientific information about the chronology of natural history. The frequent references to ancient cosmology in Genesis 1 indicate that God did not choose to reveal modern scientific information to the ancient Hebrews."[12]

---

11 Is The Bible Too Complicated For Those Who Struggle To Read? Andy Prime.
12 Ibid. Bio logos.

As previously stated, Moses' mission is to present the information in a manner where the common people can understand and share with their children. *"These commandments that I give you today are to be on your hearts. Impress them on your children. Talk about them when you sit at home and when you walk along the road, when you lie down and when you get up. Tie them as symbols on your hands and bind them on your foreheads. Write them on the door frames of your houses and on your gates."*

Seven Days

While God is not in time, He communicated the timeless events of Genesis in a manner that Moses who arrived thousands of years after the fact could record and communicate the information. The seven days represent a man's day. A day engaged in writing the events down as they were revealed by God. Writing them on stone tablets or skins would take the better part of a day or longer. Especially, when you take into account the fact that up till this point there was no written Hebrew language. Moses had to produce the written language while translating what God had given him. It seems Moses spent forty days on the mountain writing what God gave him.[13] [Miraculously quick for creating a language.] No wonder the writer told us the account of the days. Moses was spending time alone with God while He revealed to him His hinder parts.[14] We also understand the record as a man's day because it is written in a manner of the Hebrews where their day began in the evening. Thus, it was written as the evening and the morning…"[15]

---

13   Exodus Chapters 22-24
14   Exodus 33:17-23
15   Genesis 1:5

CHAPTER ONE: IN THE BEGINNING

The point of Moses' best seller is that God longed for communion. Mankind was to be the source of that intimacy. In His creation, God grew something special. We are rewarded with the information that God is pleased with His creation! Everything was good![16]

Then, God reveals to Moses that one thing was not good. The man who God created needed an enhancement. It was not going to be good for man to dwell alone. Man needed a partner. Only God could handle this challenge. Fortunately, God did not need help.

The Challenge

There was no other creature in all of God's creation that was compatible as a mate for the man. Despite wild conjecture by malevolent men, there has never been a compatible being for mankind other than the one who God was yet to create. The commandments of God to not even attempt copulation with other species is not a random thought; it is a command with serious consequences for the violators. While some have made attempts at perverting God's beautiful creation, the fact is nonetheless true. No other creature was made after the man's kind (species). God, who operates in order and pattern, had to remedy the complex problem for man while keeping him compatible with his kind.

To keep the man in the same pattern as the rest of His

---

16   Genesis 1:31

creation it was necessary to have him be able to produce "after his own kind." Moses was able, by divine revelation, to give us some of the details of this sensitive operation. God has already created the only pattern He is willing to use. He shared His image with the man. Thus, from this image He created the only compatible kind for man.

> *"And the Lord God caused a deep sleep to fall on Adam, and he slept; and He took one of his ribs and closed up the flesh in its place. Then the rib which the Lord God had taken from man He made into a woman, and He brought her to the man."*[17]

We do no damage to the objective of the text in applying a modern explanation. Explicitly, God took DNA from the man who was created in the image of God and created a woman. God does not use any of the other creatures because they are not of the same kind (species). God, in some sort of truly supernatural surgical treatment, takes the man's DNA and creates the woman. The Scripture tells us the exact area where God performed His 'surgical operation' was from his side. From the immortal man, God takes DNA and creates the immortal woman. By this process, God invites His special children (Adam and Eve) to be participatory. God has truly partnered with His creation to make man. Let us make man…[18] God created the first man. The pattern for the rest. God wanted children.[19] He partnered with His special creation to produce them. In fact, He commanded them to produce them.[20]

---

17   Genesis 2:21-22
18   Genesis 1:26.
19   2 Corinthians 6:18
20   Genesis 1:28

CHAPTER ONE: IN THE BEGINNING

Legacy

Contrary to the teaching of some, Eve was not created acquiescent to Adam. Sub servitude happens later because of sin.[21] God placed a curse on Eve and her descendants. This curse is because of her disobedience. Before the sin in the Garden, Eve is an equal partner with Adam. Like Adam, Eve is an immortal being. When God speaks of the role of the woman (before her fall from immortality), He does so in the most pleasing of terminology. *"I will make a help (or helper from the Hebrew; ezer [22]) suitable for him." The Hebrew word for helper occurs four times in this form in the Old Testament and 21 times in other forms. It most often refers to God as our helper. This is significant in that the role of helper is in no way a subservient role. Eve was not taken out of Adam's head to top him, neither out of his feet to be trampled on by him, but out of his side to be equal with him, under his arm to be protected by him, and near his heart to be loved by him. (Attributed to Matthew Henry)."* [23] The result of this performance by God is spectacular and does not go unnoticed.[24] God has given this creation, Eve, the DNA to create a heritage for her posterity. As an immortal being, Eve was unique. There is no evidence of any other immortal being (except God) with the capacity to produce other immortals! This writer often comments, "God was showing off" when He created Eve! The woman is the "crown jewel" of God's creation. Certainly, she is a sight to behold! Like the New Testament Governor of the feast,[25] God saved His best for last!

---

21   Genesis 3:16
22   https://biblehub.com/hebrew/5828.htm
23   The Legacy of Eve. Rev. Faye Reynolds.
24   Genesis 6:2
25   The Gospel of John 2:8

What a creation this woman is! She carries the seed that would give the beginning to all of those born of a woman.[26] What opportunity was afforded this special child of God. The book of Genesis does not give us a lot of fanfare about the woman. The reason is not because of God's unwillingness to showcase His special creation. Rather, it is because we are to worship the Creator and not the created!

> "God has given this creation, Eve, the DNA to create a heritage for her posterity. As an immortal being, Eve was unique."

From our vantage point we can readily understand that the woman is the central figure to the creation plan. Without the woman we have no means of achieving the nearly 8 Billion people who currently inhabit this planet. Had she not sinned there would surely be more than 100 billion people on this planet.[27] Her inauguration makes it all possible! God positioning her in His Garden is noteworthy. The garden, a place to cultivate, produces and nurtures. God made a special garden for the man and the woman. These are His special children. This has spiritual as well as natural significance.

"When the first chapter of the Bible says, 'So God created man in his own image, in the image of God he created him; male and female he created them,'[28] what is the point? The point of an image is to image. Images are erected to display the original, to point to the original, and to glorify the original. God made humans in His image

---

26   Luke 7:28
27   https://www.prb.org/howmanypeoplehaveeverlivedonearth/
28   Genesis 1:27

so the world would be filled with reflectors of God — images of God, seven billion or more statues of God. So that nobody would miss the point of creation. Nobody (unless they are stone blind) could miss the point of humanity, namely, God — knowing, loving, showing God."[29] It has been said that mankind is like a mirror image (or reflection) of the eternal God. We cannot see God but we can see His reflection.

Sons of God

The angels certainly did not miss the significance of these new kids on the block. They fully understood that these sons of God were special. Mankind were not lesser beings like the whales, apes and flies. Man was created lower than God![30] *"If this be spoken of man as he came out of the hands of his Maker, it places him at the head of all God's works; translated literally it is: Thou hast made him less than God. This is proved by his being made in the image and likeness of God, which is spoken of no other creature either in Heaven or Earth; and it is very likely that in his original creation he stood at the head of all the works of God, and next to his Maker. Obviously, higher than the angels. Is it any wonder why Satan became envious? Mankind's creation in the image of God was an announcement of a new dimension of the Holy Spirit! Man was intended by God to be something special. When, 'the angels cry, 'Holy, holy, holy is the Lord of hosts; the whole earth is full of his glory!' It's full of*

---

29   https://www.desiringgod.org/messages/why-did-god-create-the-world

30   Radu Gheorghita The Role of the Septuagint in Hebrews 2003 Page 46 "The Hebrew text is probably best construed as "you made him [man] lower than God", while the Septuagint conveys the meaning "you made him [man] lower than the angels". By using the Greek text of Ps. 8 the Author not only understood the Psalm in the translation tradition of the Septuagint, but also expounded its message by building on the particular meaning of aggelos in Ps. 8:6 LXX."

millions of human image bearers."[31] While the angels are free to cry Holy, holy, holy! They never cry Worthy, worthy, worthy! Angels do not cry worthy because only mankind knows that He is Worthy![32] Only mankind has benefited from the redemption plan of God.

"In the beginning God formed Adam, not because He was in need of humans, but so He might have someone to receive His benefits."[33] Eve is the key to accomplishing the purpose of mankind. In Genesis 1:28 God sets the purpose of Mankind for them. Then God blessed them, and God said to them, *"Be fruitful and multiply; fill the earth and subdue it; have dominion over the fish of the sea, over the birds of the air, and over every living thing that moves on the earth."* Later, another woman, Leah, said it quite well, "Behold a troop cometh."[34] Leah understood the realization of the command to be fruitful and multiply.

"In the Garden of Eden, Adam and Eve basked in the splendor of extravagant natural beauty. They were at peace and in harmony with God, each other, and all the plants and animals in Eden. The garden's provision was bountiful. Adam and Eve did not need to work hard to provide for their needs. They also had access to the Tree of Life. At any time, they could reverse the effect of wear and tear on their bodies by eating of the tree's fruit. They could enjoy optimal physical health and well-being for eternity."[35] Some say the Tree of Life was there for daily provision. It is safe to say that there was peace on Earth. The angels were excited about the earth, but it would be

---
31 Ibid. Desiring God
32 Revelation 4:8
33 Irenaeus. Against Heresies 4. 14. 1
34 Genesis 30:11
35 Why Didn't God Keep Satan Out of Eden? Hugh Ross – November 13, 2016.

millenniums before they would again see peace on the earth.[36] It is difficult to understand a time on this planet when there was peace. The sin in the Garden of Eden has negatively affected everything on Earth. In place of peace, we have had only war. In place of the Tree of Life we have had only the sting of Death. Fortunately, Jesus Christ conquered death![37]

"The good news of Jesus Christ is that the serpent's head has been crushed. The twisted lies that we can live apart from God or one another have been destroyed in the reconciling work of Jesus Christ. In reversing sin's consequences, Jesus taught us to serve one another rather than dominate. He revealed a love so deep for us that the ache in our heart for intimacy is at last filled completely in the love of Jesus. As men and women, we can once again be in a partnership dependent upon God's provisions, His grace, mercy and love. That is our true legacy as (sons and) daughters of Eve."[38] God has always been focused on His children. He often calls them sons of God.

---

36   Luke 2:14
37   I Corinthians 15
38   The Legacy of Eve. Rev. Faye Reynolds.

Chapter 2
War on mankind

"The word of the Lord came to me: 'Son of man, set your face toward Gog, of the land of Magog, the chief prince of Meshech and Tubal, and prophesy against him and say, thus says the Lord God: Behold, I am against you, O Gog, chief prince of Meshech and Tubal. And I will turn you about and put hooks into your jaws, and I will bring you out, and all your army, horses and horsemen, all of them clothed in full armor, a great host, all of them with buckler and shield, wielding swords. Persia, Cush, and Put are with them, all of them with shield and helmet; ...'" [1]

While the man and woman were enjoying the Garden of Eden like their own personal Paradise, evil forces were brooding. God placed His children in a special place He prepared for them. God obviously doted on Adam and Eve. In like manner, Jacob later preferred Joseph. Both situations would prove to foster envy. While God was pronouncing everything to be very good,[2] trouble was coming to the Garden of God.

---

1   Ezekiel 38:1-23. ESV.
2   Genesis 1:31

WAR ON EARTH

Before Genesis chapter three, there is peace on Earth. God's beautiful creation is functioning in perfect harmony. God said everything was very good! Not just good, very good! God is quite happy with His creation before the events of Genesis chapter three. God gives multiple declarations of the goodness of His creation. Those who claim that a war happened during the creation narrative need to justify their position in the context of God declaring everything very good. It is just not possible that God would have called it very good if a war was in process. The trouble must have been yet in the future or God would not have said everything was very good! In case we miss the point, the idea of very good can also be said extraordinarily, fantastically, extremely, incredibly, exceptionally, etc. God is obviously well-pleased with the standing of all His creation.

From the text it is evident that Satan is busy plotting the destruction of mankind. It is a precursor or the spark that ignites war with God. Speculation that there is a war in Heaven in the book of Genesis needs to give space to what is more likely, war on planet Earth. Before we get our focus on the proverbial war in Heaven, we must pay close attention to the events here on Earth. While theologians have imagined a war in Heaven in the first two chapters of Genesis (or before), there is no reference to such in the Scriptures. We do find war in Heaven in the book of Revelation [3] but not in Genesis. Why? From whence do theologians get their Genesis extrapolations? The idea of adding man's ideas or notions to various passages is like "reading between the lines." Using this manner of

---

3   See Chapters 12 and 19

CHAPTER TWO: WAR ON EARTH

biblical interpretation, you may come to literally any conclusion. This kind of biblical interpretation is dangerous. False elucidation is the root of all false doctrines.

The information available to us about Heavenly matters or wars is scant in comparison to the information we have about events here on Earth. Let us see if we can discern what happened in God's exceptionally good creation. The theologians could quite possibly be 'warm' in their search of the proper application of the war in Heaven first mentioned by Apostle John by hoping to find it somewhere in Genesis. When Satan enacts his plan, it is a declaration of war on mankind. War on God, war on Earth and war on the supernatural realm. All are implicated in Satan's treachery. While many speak of the so-called supernatural, we must know assuredly that God is the only truly Supernatural being. All others are created beings. Offers of supernatural abilities from other than God are the same as what Satan offered Eve.

Apostle James helps us understand the path to sin. *"Then, when desire has conceived, it gives birth to sin; and sin, when it is full-grown, brings forth death."* [4] It may not be easy to ascertain the point when desire is conceived, but when it gives birth to sin it is generally much more visible. Sin is an action word. So, when did Satan sin? When did Satan's actions (sin) incite war on Earth? The sin of Satan was premeditated and intentional. Most often people place all the blame for sin solely on Satan. However, Satan had a few willing accomplices. While it is true that without Satan there would not

---

4   James 1:15

have been sin on Earth. The fact remains that there is a Satan and he started war here on Earth. The result of the activity in Genesis is war between Satan, his angels, and their God. The number of those former angels who join Satan's conspiracy against God is not known. It may be that it was not initially revealed which angels had conceived sin in their hearts. We also do not know the total number of God's angels. It is not given to us to know. War in Heaven is a theme of the book of Revelation, but the events that precipitated the war in Heaven ostensibly started here on Earth long before the book of Revelation was received and written by the Apostle John.

The angels were previously shouting for joy at God's creation. Now, some have chosen to be God's enemies. There must be a reason for such a radical departure! We may venture that the source of this discontent rests somewhere in the creation epic. Nowhere in the story of creation do we find mention of any other creatures except the ones that God creates for Earth. The fact that the angels are not included in the narrative may be more telling than we realize.

The primary reason that there is not more mention of angels in Scripture is because the Scriptures were not written to or for angels. The Scriptures were written for mankind, particularly fallen, mortal man. We know this because most of the topics deal with men after they had fallen or about mankind's fall from immortality to mortal. All of the Bible was written after man fell from immortality. When we say "fallen man," we are inferring mortality. Before the sin in the garden mankind was immortal. After their sin, Adam and

Eve became mortal. One of the horrors of those who are mortal is physical death. Incidentally, the Scriptures were not only written for mankind, they were written down by mankind as moved by the Holy Ghost. Thus, man's message has the imprimatur of Almighty God. He saw no need to give more attention to angels.

The other reason that the Genesis epic does not focus on angels is that our worship, our veneration, and attention are intended for God. God is a jealous God [5] when it comes to our attention. He was careful not to allow mankind to be confused about to whom we owe allegiance. In His diligence He made daily visits to our first parents. "Let all the angels of God worship Him."[6]

Eden: The Garden Of God

Eden means paradise.[7] Eden was an area of land and within this area was a special garden that God had planted. Some scholars project that the Garden of God (Garden of Eden) was the dwelling place of God. *"The river that flows out of Eden and into the garden is no ordinary river. Ordinary rivers have tributaries that feed water into them, but this river runs the opposite way: it feeds water into four other rivers which supply water to all directions of the realm. Eden is the source of provision, the head of the life-giving water that nourishes the realm. Eden is the fountain of providence, the torrential spring that flows from the sovereign to sustainl Life in his realm."*[8]

---

5 Exodus 34:14
6 Hebrews 1:6
7 https://www.merriam-webster.com/dictionary/paradise
8 Was Eden God's Palace? Alan Browne. May 11, 2016

If Eden still exists, it is safe to say that it is not in this realm. Mankind does not have access to the Garden of God. There is no place on Earth where five rivers all meet in one location! The potential for life in such an environment is extraordinary.

"Right in the middle of the garden is another symbol of the sovereign's life-giving provision for His subjects: The Tree of ife.[9] Taken together, all these provisions suggest that Eden is the earthly dwelling of the Heavenly sovereign. The king not only constructed this realm; he provides everything to sustain life in His realm. Eden is therefore the palace of the great king - not a physical building made of stones, but the dwelling-place of the sovereign who oversees and takes care of his earthly realm."[10]

Almighty God may have more than one special place, but it is certain that Eden was one of them. *"If we understand 'Eden' as the dwelling-place of the divine sovereign, then "the garden of Eden" is the visually stunning and providentially nourishing landscape associated with Eden—the grounds of the palace. Together, Eden and its garden form a picture of the Heavenly sovereign living among his subjects. This theme—the Heavenly sovereign dwelling among humans—is central to the whole Biblical narrative."[11]* *"Some scholars talk about Eden as a temple. Eden is the original ideal of God living among His people, and that ideal is re-expressed in the tabernacle, in Solomon's temple, and so on."[12]* The theme of a dwelling place for God carries into the New Testament where Apostle Paul said that we are the temple of

---

9   Genesis 2:9
10   Ibid. Browne.
11   Ibid. Browne.
12   Ibid. Browne

the Holy Ghost![13]

If indeed Eden was the original palace, then the Throne of God, the presence of angels and more makes perfect sense to be in this utopian Kingdom. Here God plants a special garden and in this garden, God placed His special creation. His children were the very likeness of Him, Adam and Eve. Made in His likeness (image). Angels were present in this area but access to Adam and Eve was not authorized to angels. Adam and Eve were treated as mirror images of their creator. Certainly, angels could be nearby, but they were not in direct communication. They were welcome to tour God's creation, but angels were of a different kind (species). Beings from another realm did not engage in conversations with God's special children. The angel's domain was to serve the One on the throne. Mankind's job was similar, but we might see it more as "in development." In all cases there is a penalty for disobedience.'

> *"For the Lord your God in your midst is a jealous God—lest the anger of the Lord your God be kindled against you, and destroy you from off the face of the earth."*[14]

Notice the penalty for disobedience is referenced in the language of the obliteration. The same God who brought a great flood on the earth to destroy those who did not keep Him first, will do similar to those who fail to keep Him in His proper place. Similar language is used throughout Scripture. Serve the Lord with all your

---
13 I Corinthians 6:19
14 Deuteronomy 6:15

heart and wonderful things will happen, including eternal life! Serve Satan's path of sin (rebellion against God's commandments) and you will die forever.[15]

"And so we have the prophetic word confirmed, which you do well to heed as a light that shines in a dark place, until the day dawns and the morning star rises in your hearts; knowing this first, that no prophecy of Scripture is of any private interpretation, for prophecy never came by the will of man, but holy men of God spoke as they were moved by the Holy Spirit."[16]

Everyone Is Not Happy That God Made Mankind In His Image

While the angels were busy doing angel assignments, Genesis chapter three abruptly introduces a being that is obviously not exhilarated with God's newest creation. This is the first indication readers of Genesis have of these beings. This being is an angel destined to become more notorious than any other. This angel's reaction to God's "very good" creation assessment develops into quite a departure from the public reception most of the angels had given to God on the subject.

What is this being doing in the Garden of Eden? We know that he was granted access to this paradise because, like all the angels, he was a committed servant of God. It does not seem like Satan received special treatment. We should ask what held Satan's interest that he apparently made multiple trips to the Garden?[17]

---

15 Deuteronomy chapter 28
16 2 Peter 1:19-21
17 Ezekiel 28:13

Ezekiel's declaration "you were in Eden, the garden of God" lends us to wonder if Eden was also home to this being. *"This also is a strong irony. Thou art like Adam, when in his innocence and excellence he was in the garden of Eden! Thou art the anointed cherub that covereth - The irony is continued; and here he is likened to the Cherub that guarded the gates of Paradise (Eden), and kept the way of the Tree of Life; or to one of the cherubs whose wings, spread out, covered the mercy-seat."*[18] This points to Satan in a light we rarely consider. Notice that God responds to the sin in the Garden by releasing His angel army (Cherubim) in Eden to defend the way to the Tree of Life. We must consider this to be in response to Satan's role with such an elite group.

Planning the Deception

Why was Satan so focused on getting on this stage with Eve? It was a stage that was not in his realm. Satan likes to pretend he is above mankind.[19] If Satan was really above mankind would he care about the two people in the Garden? Even Satan knows that he was created lower than mankind.

The angels, like mankind, are afforded choice. It is easy to wonder, *"Why did God let Satan pull off this hoax?"* Didn't God know that Satan was about to sin? We might also ask the same about Eve. Did God know that Eve was going to sin? Why did He not just stop her? God knew. God knows we might sin. He is not going to stop us from sinning. This is a choice. There will nonetheless be a penalty for our transgressions.

---

18   Adam Clark Commentary Exodus 28:13
19   Isaiah 14:13-14

The all-knowing God is aware of Satan's visits to the Garden of God.[20] No surprise there. We should inquire, "what is Satan's objective in confusing Eve?" What we know about the serpent is very little and in fairness the passage in Genesis does not give us much information. Most of what we learn about the serpent we learn much later, primarily from Isaiah and Ezekiel. However, if we pay careful attention to the text, we will learn all we really need to understand at this point. Although it is clearly not in the text, we imagine that Satan was buddies with Adam and Eve! While Satan may have a "frequent flyer" card for visits to the Garden of Eden, we need to understand that these were not visits to Adam and Eve. Adam and Eve were in the Garden of God and Satan may have been there as well. However, there was no communication. Adam and Eve's communication was with God — not with angels.[21] Satan was not on Adam and Eve's guest list.

Satan used his visits to set the trap for his ultimate manipulation of the 'serpent' and surrounding operations. Satan needed a way to manifest so that he could communicate with God's special children. He needed a medium. A creature that was already in communication with Eve would be ideal. We know that Satan had to use some form of manipulation or deception to accomplish his plan. Satan was not from this realm so he had no body. He sought a way to "appear" because, like all angels, he is a spirit, he had no body.[22] So, he formed a plan to co-opt some unfortunate creature to support in his scheme.

---

20   Psalm 139
21   Isaiah 14:13-14
22   Hebrews 1:14

CHAPTER TWO: WAR ON EARTH

Mankind was not created for the angels, which is the reason why we have no mention of the angels in the creation narrative. Mankind was created by God for God. If there were interactions with angels before the tragedy of Genesis chapter three, God would have included such in His narrative. The angels could only observe what was happening. Angels were not a part of the proceedings on Earth.

Angels are from a different realm than mankind. We do not even know if they can actually speak like men unless given some special circumstantial privilege by God, much like Balaam's donkey. We assume angels speak because of God allowing several incidents of angels bringing messages to men. Those may be special manifestations that God granted under unique circumstances.

Entering Stage Left

Envision the Garden of Eden like a stage play. The angels were permitted to be a part of the audience, but they have no role in the production. Angels had no permission and no means of direct communication with mankind. Like cheerleaders standing on the sidelines cheering, but not a part of the game. What kind of conversation would an angel need to have with a man anyway? Unless, of course, God sent the angel. This is one of many areas where mankind has allowed themselves to get caught up in Satan's schemes. We do not worship angels!

Satan decided he wanted to be a part of the production. His lust to be "on the stage" was driving him to find a way to communicate with mankind. Permission was needed. That was not a path that would work for Satan. There was a problem here that would be reflected throughout the history of mankind. How could a creature from another realm communicate with mankind? God had separated them for a reason. Some theologians have erroneously postulated that Satan in his state before his fall could somehow communicate directly to mankind in the state they were in before the fall of man. They propose that for Adam and/or Eve communicating with the angelic host was a normal, regular activity. This is not factual. There is no Scripture to support such philosophies. Adam and Eve were not in regular communication with angelic beings before or even after their fall from immortality to mere mortals. The only being that they communicated with was God! This communication was intimate and daily until they sinned. I understand that this is hard to imagine in a world filled with so many messages and most of them from our adversary the devil.[23]

It is true that there are later incidents where angels communicate with mankind, but these are very few and with the direct imprimatur of God. God had open communication with mankind before Adam and Eve rebelled, but afterward God is presented with a challenge. How does He communicate with fallen man? Man, because of his transgressions against God, is no longer a participant with those who are partakers of the Tree of Life. Fortunately for all of us, God has a plan for our redemption and He immediately begins to enact it.

---

[23]   I Peter 5:8.

Chapter 3
Theophany and Christophany

"God, who at various times and in various ways spoke in time past to the fathers by the prophets, has in these last days spoken to us by His Son, whom He has appointed heir of all things, through whom also He made the worlds; who being the brightness of His glory and the express image of His person, and upholding all things by the word of His power, when He had by Himself purged our sins, sat down at the right hand of the Majesty on high, having become so much better than the angels, as He has by inheritance obtained a more excellent name than they."[1]

To communicate with His alienated children, God employs a plethora of methods. *"The writer of Hebrews summarizes that God appeared at various times, by various persons, in various laws and forms of teaching, with various degrees of clearness, under various shadows, types, and figures, and with various modes of revelation, such as by angels, visions, dreams, mental impressions, etc."*[2] There could be no better explanation of

---

1   Hebrews 1:1-4
2   Joseph Benson's Commentary of the Old and New Testaments. Hebrews 1

how theophanies fit into God's perfect plan for the redemption of mankind. *"Under the New Testament, all is done by One, i.e. Jesus Christ."*[3]

The word "theophany" is a combination of two Greek words, meaning God and appearance.[4] "More precisely, it is a visible display to mankind that expresses the presence and character of God. Examples include:

- The thunderous display at the top of Mount Sinai (Ex.19)

- The burning bush (Ex.3)

- Appearances to Abraham (Gen. 15:1; 17:1; 18:1)

- Isaac (Gen. 26:2)

- Jacob (Gen. 28:13)

- The cloud of fire in the wilderness (Ex. 14:19; 40:34; Num. 9:15-23

- Micaiah's vision (1 Kings 22:19-22)

- Isaiah's vision (Isaiah 6)

- Ezekiel's vision (Ezek. 1)

- John's vision of God on His throne (Rev. 4-5)"[5]

---

3   Joseph Benson's Commentary of the Old and New Testaments. Heb. 1
4   10 Things You Should Know about Theophanies. Vern S. Poythress. February 11, 2018
5   Ibid. Poythress.

CHAPTER THREE: THEOPHANY AND CHRISTOPHANY

"Christophany comes from two Greek words; Christos, which means Christ, and phaneroo, which means to be revealed or to manifest. Therefore, a Christophany is a visible manifestation or appearance of Christ before His human incarnation. It's kind of like Stan Lee's cameo appearances in Marvel movies."[6] You get to see the Creator in a cameo appearance, the Lord Himself![7] Jesus Christ has multiple cameo appearances before His grand entrance as the Son of Man. If you understand that Jesus Christ was not another God but rather a manifestation of the one true God, the Creator of the Universe, then either of the two words theophany or Christophany is applicable.

The Angel of the Lord

The Bible speaks of this dignitary called the "angel of the LORD." Also referred to as the "angel of the Presence" or the "angel or messenger, of the Covenant." He appears in many important contexts in Scripture. The manner in which He is described sets Him apart from all the other angels.[8] It is clear to the reader that this is something more than just an angel.

"One of the most persuasive arguments for Scripture's legitimacy is the fact that as the story progresses, it sheds light on what came before. Throughout the New Testament, we are introduced to principles and concepts that illuminate passages that were not entirely clear or obvious. This happens in the form of theophanies — physical manifestations of God that we can now recognize as being Jesus. The Old Testament's angel of the Lord is a perfect example of a

---

6   wordsoffaithhopelove.com/jesus-in-the-old-testament-christophanies/
7   I Thessalonians 4:16
8   blueletterbible.org/faq/don_stewart/don_stewart_26.cfm

theophany. When you begin to look closer at this biblical figure, you recognize three crucial truths that identify this character as Jesus."[9] *"On a number of occasions in the Old Testament when the angel of the LORD appeared, it seems to be the LORD Himself. The angel has attributes that belong to God and God alone. In addition, He is addressed as the LORD. If this be the case, then He is not a created being."*[10] The Angel of the Lord is a manifestation of God. For God to manifest as a man is a quite different matter than an angel doing similar. For God, man was made in His image so for Him to manifest as a man is rather easy and of course He is God! The appearances of the angel of the Lord were manifestations of Jesus before His incarnation. Jesus declared Himself to be existent "before Abraham."[11] It is logical that He would be active and manifest in the world. Whatever the case, whether the angel of the Lord was a pre-incarnate appearance of Christ (Christophany) or an appearance of God the Father (theophany), it is highly likely that the phrase 'the angel of the Lord' usually identifies a physical appearance of God.[12] Other times, however, the angel of the LORD is clearly distinguished from the LORD. On these occasions the angel must be a created being rather than God Himself. *"The appearances of the angel of the Lord cease after the incarnation of Christ. Angels are mentioned numerous times in the New Testament, but 'the angel of the Lord' is never mentioned in the New Testament after the birth of Christ."*[13]

In Balaam's account, the Angel of the Lord meets Balaam. The Angel of the Lord is visible to the donkey but not to Balaam. Instead,

---

9   Who Is the Angel of the Lord? Jayson Bradley | Mar 26, 2019
10   Ibid.
11   John 8:58
12   gotquestions.org/angel-of-the-Lord.html
13   gotquestions.org/angel-of-the-Lord.html

CHAPTER THREE: THEOPHANY AND CHRISTOPHANY

God speaks through the donkey as though it was speaking to Balaam. Then, the Angel of the Lord opens Balaam's eyes and he is able to see the Angel of the Lord who has His sword drawn.[14] The donkey seems to have better sense of the situation than the man does.

Melchizedek

Melchizedek is without doubt a Christophany. The Lord is called by David "a priest forever after the order of Melchizedek."[15] The writer of Hebrews said Melchizedek was *"without father, without mother, without descent, having neither beginning of days, nor end of life; but made like unto the Son of God; abideth a priest continually."*[16] The usual interpretation of these words is that he was made into a type of Christ since, as a "King of Righteousness" (meaning of Melchizedek) and "King of Peace."[17] As King of Peace, He would seem to be superior in rank to the Prince of Peace unless of course they were both God. We know that princes usually are on a path to kingship. The Prince of Peace of the Old Testament becomes King of Peace in the New Testament. It is evident that there is only one King of Peace and that is certainly the Mighty God who manifested Himself and dwelt among mankind.[18]

Melchizedek appears suddenly, with no mention of either ancestry or death. This could only be applicable to Christ Himself

---

14   Numbers chapter 22
15   Psalm 110:4, Hebrews 5:6, 10; 6:20; 7:1-21
16   Hebrews 7:3
17   Ibid. Bradley.
18   1 Timothy 3:16

appearing to Abram in a theophany. This would also solve the problem of how such a godly king and priest as Melchizedek could be ruling a city in such an ungodly land as Canaan and why, if he did, Abram would have had no other contact with him. The fact that He was "made like unto the Son of God" accords with one of Christ's pre-incarnate appearances; at His birth, He became the incarnate Son of God forever.

Melchizedek was also said to be a man,[19] but the same is true with other theophanies, one of which was likewise manifested to Abram and Lot.[20] Melchizedek's Salem could never have been Jerusalem is evident especially from Ezekiel 16:2–4.[21]

Michael The Archangel

At first glance, it might seem that Michael is just another angel or maybe a little more important one. However, we are privileged to know this one's name. This is unique. Scripture only gives us a proper name of one other angel and who knows, there may be more to that than we understand. That angel is Gabriel. "We're told Michael's title in Jude 9. The Greek word for 'archangel' (archággelos) means 'chief angel' or 'chief messenger.'"

"The word 'archangel' is not used to describe him in the Old Testament, but another angel calls him one of the chief princes."[22] "Michael only says four

---

19   Hebrews 7:4
20   Genesis 18:2,22; 19:1-24
21   https://www.icr.org/books/defenders/341
22   6 biblical facts about Michael the archangel. Jeffrey Kranz See Daniel

CHAPTER THREE: THEOPHANY AND CHRISTOPHANY

words in the Bible. Well, three Greek words that are often translated into four English words. Michael says to Satan, 'The Lord rebuke you!'[23] Calling Michael 'one of the chief princes' implies that Michael has peers. However, if there are any other archangels, the Bible doesn't tell us. In Scripture there is only one reference to an archangel." Study will show that Michael is way more than just another angel. In the book of Daniel chapter ten, we read of the Prophet Daniel being perplexed. In response to his perplexity, he begins a fast that lasts 21 days. Then, God comes on the scene. In this passage we see the angel Michael mentioned and this causes some to misunderstand.

Daniel 10:5-6 and Revelation 1:13-15 are companion passages. Ezekiel chapter one and ten give a similar description. *"A careful comparison of the descriptions given in these passages of Scripture identifies the individual pictured in them as the same being. The 'man' of dazzling brightness in Daniel 10 is clearly Jesus Christ."*[24] Who alone can defeat Satan? Who came to help Gabriel in his struggle against the prince of evil? The answer is Michael. There is a great deal of misinterpretation in the Christian world on the identity of Michael. Just who is this Michael? What does his name mean? The name Michael means one who is like God.[25] We know that there is really no one like God except God. The only way for Michael to be like God is for Him to be God or be a son of God. Angels are not sons — never in Scripture.

10:13

23   Ibid. Kranz.

24   https://www.itiswritten.com/unsealing-daniels-mysteries-les- son-10-with-

25   Ibid. It is written.

So, Michael must be the former — which is God! *"Michael is mentioned only five times in the Bible. Besides Daniel 10:13, 21, the other references to Michael are found in:*

- *Michael commands the angels and has the authority to cast Satan out of Heaven.[26]*

- *Michael has the authority to raise Moses from the dead.[27]*

- *Michael delivers His people in the time of trouble and has the power to resurrect the dead.[28]*

- *Angels do not have the power to resurrect the dead. Such power rests only in Jesus Christ.[29]*

These verses clearly reveal that Michael is one of the many names of Jesus. Jesus is the Lamb, the Lion, the Rock of Ages, the Lily of the Valley, the Rose of Sharon, the Door, the Way, the Truth and the Life. When Scripture uses the term, "Michael," to refer to Jesus, it reveals Christ as the "Mighty Conqueror." Don't let the expression, "Michael the Archangel,"[30] confuse you. The word, "archangel," means the "commander and chief" of the angels. Jesus is not an angel."[31] He is the manifestation of God in flesh. "He never

---

26 Revelation 12:7-9
27 Jude 9
28 Daniel 12:1, 2
29 Matthew 28:19
30 Jude 9
31 Ibid. It is written.

CHAPTER THREE: THEOPHANY AND CHRISTOPHANY

had a beginning and will never have an ending.[32] He is eternal.[33] He existed before the angels[34] and created them."[35]

> "...Now when Joshua was near Jericho, he looked up and saw a man standing in front of him with a drawn sword in his hand. Joshua went up to him and asked, "Are you for us or for our enemies?" "Neither," he replied, "but as commander of the army of Jehovah I have now come." Then Joshua fell face-down to the ground in reverence, and asked him, "What message does my Lord have for his servant?" The commander of the Lord's army replied, "Take off your sandals, for the place where you are standing is holy."[36]

Jesus is described as a sword wielding Captain or Commander of GOD's army. This again indicates Jesus is Michael. Remember, He is presented to Joshua in a manner that Joshua presumes Him an angel, but God sets the record straight.

> "As the Commander and Chief of the angels, Jesus breaks through the sky with the voice of 'the archangel.'" The righteous dead are resurrected. The righteous living, along with the righteous dead, are changed into glorious, immortal beings. Together, they ascend into the Heavens to meet their triumphant Lord."[37] Michael is obviously a theophany of Jesus Christ.

Why did He appear? [*There was a problem.*] "The prince of

32	Revelation 1:8
33	John 8:58
34	Hebrews 1:3-4
35	Ibid. It is written.
36	Joshua 5:13-15
37	Ibid. It is written.

the Kingdom of Persia withstood Gabriel.[38] Who is the 'Prince of this world' and the 'Prince of the power of the air?'" These are

> *"There are theologians who fall into error and teach that Satan is an archangel."*

both descriptions of Satan. When God created Adam and Eve, He gave them dominion over the earth. When they decided to follow Satan's advice, they lost their dominion. "Adam was no longer earth's Prince, and Eve was no longer a Princess. They became servants—slaves of the one they had obeyed.[39] Satan usurped their position. He now became the "Prince of this world."[40] As such, he is referred to as "the Prince of the Kingdom of Persia."[41]

Is Satan An Archangel?

There are theologians who fall into error and teach that Satan is an archangel. Satan has sold his illusions into our minds. Not much personal information about Satan is given in the biblical texts. Satan and the devil are titles meaning resistor and tempter, and not necessarily specific to this angel. Some exterior texts hint at his name and the names of his compatriots. These are more clever attempts by Satan to infiltrate the sons of God. There is also no indication in the Bible that Satan is the most powerful or even has more power than any of the other angels, even though he is the leader. There may be demon princes/chieftains as powerful or more powerful than him in terms of strength, we do not know, but he is the leader.

---

38   John 12:31; Ephesians 2:2, 3
39   Romans 6:16
40   John 16:11
41   Ibid. It is written.

Chapter 4
Who is satan?

"I call Heaven and earth to witness against you today, that I have set before you life and death, blessing and curse. Therefore choose life, that you and your offspring may live." [1]

The original Hebrew term śāṭān (Hebrew: שָׂטָן) is a noun meaning "accuser" or "adversary."[2] The Hebrew Bible uses the word to refer to both human adversaries,[3] and a specific supernatural entity.[4] The word is derived from a verb meaning primarily "to obstruct, oppose." When it is used without the definite article (simply satan), the word can refer to any accuser, but when it is used with the

---

1   Deuteronomy 30:19
2   Kelly, Henry Ansgar (2006), Satan: A Biography, Cambridge, England: Cambridge University Press, ISBN 978-0521604024
3   Campo, Juan Eduardo (2009), "Satan", Encyclopedia of Islam, New York City: Infobase Publishing, pp. 603–604, ISBN 978-0-8160-5454-1
4   Ibid. Campo.

definite article (ha-satan), it usually refers specifically to the Heavenly accuser: the satan."[5] In this writing, we have opted to use Satan as a general designation for all activities related to Satan and his angels. The word Satan does not occur in the Book of Genesis. Instead, we have reference to the creature that Satan manipulated. This creature is referred to as the serpent.[6] The first occurrence of the word "satan" is related to Balaam.[7]

Satan Is Not a Man

In our popular culture Satan is usually betrayed as some sort of man or manlike personage. Satan is not a man. Another popular way that Satan is portrayed is as some sort of a modern interpretation of angels.

While Satan is indeed an angel, we must remember that no one knows how an angel looks. Thus, artist renditions of angels should not be considered accurate. Make no mistake, Satan would love to be a man. However, Satan is not of the same species as mankind. Satan is angel kind. Satan was created an angel. So, he will always be of that kind. Angel kind do not become humankind and humankind do not become angel kind. Just as God said in the beginning, everything is created after its own kind; that will not change. Speculation that Satan could have simply came to Adam and Eve looking like a man is senseless. There are several reasons:

---

5   Ibid. Campo.
6   Kelly, Henry Ansgar (2006), Satan: A Biography, Cambridge, England: Cambridge University Press, ISBN 978-0521604024
7   Numbers 22:22

CHAPTER FOUR: WHO IS SATAN?

- There were no other men (or women). Adam and Eve were in innocence – not ignorance. Adam and Eve would have seen right through a ruse of a being posing as a man and question why such a thing was happening since they knew they were the only people.

    a. It may be that the art of manifesting requires something that actually exists. This is an area where we have very limited understanding. Yet, the serpent was an existing creature.

    b. Satan could manifest or manipulate as some creature. He could not manifest as a man. Man is made in the image of God. There is no place in Scripture where Satan manifested as a being that looked like a man.

- Man was created in the image of God. For an angel to take it upon itself to assume such a form would certainly require permission and without permission would certainly violate the law of God. The Scripture teaches us that Satan can manifest as an angel of light.[8] This is not suggesting that he may appear in the image of a man, it merely speaks to his character as a master deceiver. "The Apostle had the history of the temptation and fall of man particularly in view. He refers to the same thing. In whatever form Satan appeared to our first mother, he pretended that Eve should get a great increase of light, that is, wisdom and understanding, he deceived her, and led her to transgress."[9] Apparently, this is the first in a

---

[8] 2 Cor. 11:14
[9] Adam Clarke Commentary. 2 Cor. 11:14

series of billions of unfulfilled promises to bring light by the self-proclaimed light-bringer! Satan was one of God's angels until the point where he enacted his sinful plot. The Apostle is warning us to use all caution and discernment of spirits lest we also be deceived.

- There is no Scripture to support the idea that Satan can appear in the image of a man (i.e. in the image of God).

- Taking on the form of a being created in the image of God would certainly get the attention of the all-knowing God. Satan was not looking for permission; he was focused on deception. His plan was premeditated.

- Being made in the image of God is a big deal! Only one being is created in the image of God and that is mankind! All others are easily exposed as imposters.

- There is spiritual danger in granting Satan power that is not his. Remember there is no evidence that he has any special power. He is an angel, but not a god. The leader of angels but not more powerful than any other angel.

Mankind was not only created in the image of God. God created them to rule.[10] "Them?" —as in Adam and Eve. No other being had been given such authority. Ruler ship was granted only to God's special children. At the time of Genesis that was Adam and Eve's domain. No one else was in their exclusive club. Perhaps the clause where God chides Satan, "Have you considered my servant

---

10   Genesis 1:26-27

CHAPTER FOUR: WHO IS SATAN?

Job?" is reflective of God's desired expectation of all His special children, His sons. Job, the righteous, one of the sons of God.

Wild suppositions on communicating with other species are not new. Supposing someone wanted to communicate with another species. How would they accomplish such a feat? Suppose a man wanted to communicate with ants. The best way to accomplish this would to become an ant. If one could voluntarily change and become reborn as an ant, that would give him the ability to communicate with the ants. A mere man attempting communication with ants is beyond our capability and totally out of our realm. Science fiction has resolved this challenge with the Antman, but we are speaking here in reality.

What we understand of this serpent is that he is somehow a manifestation or is manipulated by Satan. Satan could not become a man so he manipulated a creature that could communicate with Eve. What would cause Satan to violate one of God's created animals in such a way? Envy is a very powerful motivator. Cain envied Abel and the result is Cain murdered his brother. Satan envied Eve and the result was a plan to murder all of her offspring. There are some horrible mass murderers in history. These did the work of their father the devil. Yet, none of them can match the death toll that Satan has amassed in his mission to kill the children of Adam and Eve. He alone stands as the most despicable tempter in all of history.

"Let no one say when he is tempted, "I am tempted by God"; for God cannot be tempted by evil, nor does He Himself tempt anyone. But each one is tempted when

he is drawn away by his own desires and enticed. Then, when desire has conceived, it gives birth to sin; and sin, when it is fullgrown, brings forth death."[11]

The Serpent

Adolf Hitler famously said, *"If you tell a big enough lie and tell it frequently enough, it will be believed."* He was right about that, and his theory stated that it would be believed because no one could imagine someone distorting truth so terribly. Satan's lie was a big one — a direct contradiction to what God said. *"You will NOT die."*[12]

"Often, people say that they can't believe the serpent in Genesis 3 spoke because they claim animals don't speak! Well, I wish I could tell that to my sister-in-law's Blue-Fronted Amazon Parrot that doesn't stop talking! Many types of parrots talk by mimicking, so it would be illogical to think that God didn't give this ability to other animals—especially in a perfect world. Speaking human sounding words and speaking intelligently, however, is not the same. Balaam's donkey, as the only other example given of animals speaking in Scripture, was specially enabled by the power of God to speak intelligently to Balaam."[13] In the case of the donkey, it was God Himself speaking. This does not mean that either creature (the serpent or donkey) was gifted with the ability to think and then turn those thought patterns into speech. These were merely manifestations allowing thought to be verbalized. In both cases, the point was to send a message to

---

11   James 1:13-15
12   https://www.ttil.tv/three-tactics-satan-used-to-fool-eve
13   Shouldn't the Woman (Eve) Have Been Shocked that a Serpent Spoke? Satan, the Fall, and a Look at Good and Evil. Bodie Hodge. February 2, 2010.

CHAPTER FOUR: WHO IS SATAN?

mankind. In both cases, the message was received and understood.

> "Because there is no other place in Scripture that reveals Satan or demons can grant animals the ability to speak, it makes more sense that the serpent could make the sounds capable of speech and Satan used this to his advantage. In essence, Satan likely used this feature that the original serpent had and caused it to say what he wanted. Although this may sound far-fetched here should be caution about limiting what God did or did not do in the perfect Garden. Many animals have types of sound-based or mimicry forms of communication today."[14]

> "How does a serpent, created good by God, intentionally tempt Adam and Eve and lead them into rebellion against God? Again, it is important to point out that the Bible is not explicit here. But several key passages suggest that Satan inhabited the serpent and used it as his instrument to deceive Adam and Eve."[15] "Passages like Matthew 8:28–34 and Mark 5:6-13 indicate demons can inhabit both people and animals. Luke 22:3 shows us that Satan, at least on one occasion, 'entered into' a man and used him as his instrument to betray Jesus. Revelation 12:9 and John 8:44 offer proof that the serpent of the garden is none other than Satan himself."[16] The serpent approached Eve without in any way catching her by surprise. If this was the first, she had ever seen of a serpent, Eve would at least have been a little surprised by its presence."[17]

Do not forget that Eve lived in the world's first and perhaps largest zoological garden. As such she likely knew more about animals

---

14   Ibid. Bodie Hodge.
15   Ibid. Richard.
16   Ibid. Richard.
17   Where Did Satan Come From? NOVEMBER 15, 2018 | GUY M. RICHARD

than anyone else in history. Likely Noah would be in the running for top animal expert! Nonetheless, Eve was accustomed to animals of all types. *"... the serpent was 'clever' when it spoke. It made sense to the woman.[18] Since satan was the one who influenced the serpent,[19] then it makes sense the serpent could deliver a cogent message capable of deceiving her. The serpent apparently cooperated and was an instrument in the deception and so deserved a punishment, which God justly administered. This reminds us of Judas, who also received due punishment, even though Satan entered him."[20]*

"The devil made me do it," is not an acceptable justification. Serpents don't speak, but the curse[21] probably was somehow related to the activity. Here is some good advice. If you encounter a talking serpent, RUN! We do not know how loud the creature spoke. It may have been a whisper. It is conceivable that it whispered in Eve's ear, which may explain why we have no record of it communicating with Adam. Satan, the master of whispering, may well have remained hidden from Eve for the whole exchange. Satan is not from the realm of mankind so not being visible is in his realm.

"In Genesis 3, the serpent is an actual creature. It is not to be understood as an allegory or as a representation of some other type of creature. This was an actual being who was with Adam and Eve in the Garden of Eden. Scripture nowhere gives any indication for this story to be understood symbolically." It seems clear from Scripture

---

18   When using "Woman" in caps, this denotes Eve's original name as given in Genesis 2:23, when Adam named her. She was originally named Woman and it seems wasn't given the name Eve until after sin.

19   Revelation 12:9, 20:2

20   Luke 22:3

21   Genesis 3:14

that there was an actual serpent in the Garden. He (or it) is described as one of the wild animals God had made."[22] The serpent was not a supernatural being. Satan entered into the body (or appeared to enter) of the serpent to tempt Adam and Eve. Therefore, Satan himself is the personage behind the serpent. The serpent was the instrument the devil used to do his bidding. Thus, we can conclude that the tempter was the devil who was disguised in the form of an animal.[23] Satan loves deception.

Like the scenario of Satan manifesting as a man, there are questions about this "use a creature approach." We can speculate but it is apparent that whatever this creature was, it must have been like the family pet. It had to have functioned in such a manner that it already had the trust of Adam and Eve, or at least Eve. It is not too hard to imagine that a creature could be a family pet. The list of family pets is endless and range from rats to crocodiles to elephants. Whatever this creature was, it is apparent that it did not need permission to interact with Adam and Eve. The point that it began to talk may seem strange but certainly not out of the realm of possibility. "How cute," Eve may have thought it was when the creature began to speak to her.

Other than birds, the African elephant, the Beluga whale, and the harbor seal have all been documented to mimic speech. *"The undisputed champion of speech mimicry was an African Gray parrot named Alex. He was trained by cognitive scientist Irene Pepperberg of Harvard University in Cambridge, Massachusetts. Alex could quickly learn and imitate*

---

22   Genesis 1:25; 2:19
23   blueletterbible.org/faq/don_stewart/don_stewart_705.cfm

new English words. He could even say, 'I love you' and wished Pepperberg good night after a hard day's training."[24]

"The great Jewish Rabbis and sages of long ago point to something rather interesting in verse 1 about the serpent: the serpent was different from the wild animals God had created; he wasn't even one of the wild animals."[25] The implication is that whatever the type of creature, this serpent was apparently domesticated — perhaps the family pet. The Scriptures say, the verse says, "Than any wild animal." Apparently, the serpent was not even categorized as a wild animal. The serpent was unique...a separate and distinct living being..."[26]

Deceiver

Satan means deceiver. Scripture later reveals he was the beneficiary of favor from God, Even so, the events of Genesis three show us that he becomes the enemy of God when he commits an act of war against His Kingdom. Those deceived become dangerous to themselves and to others. When Satan asks, "Hath God said?" We know he is asking the question of Eve. Yet, it might also be that he is struggling with the question himself. Will sin actually bring physical death to mankind? Bear in mind, there was no death previous to this; death was a mystery. Much like the promise to destroy the earth with rain, it was an unknown.[27] Those who sin often wrestle with their actions until they make the impasse. It is apparent that Satan

---

24   bbc.com/earth/story/20150216-can-any-animals-talk-like-humans
25   torahclass.com/old-testament-studies-tc/34-old-testament-studies-genesis/79-lesson-4-genesis-3-4
26   Ibid.
27   Genesis 2:5-6.

is planning rebellion. Those who embrace sin love company. Satan enlisted help as he grappled with his deception. Is it even possible that he joined Eve and then Adam in tasting the fruit of the tree of know ledge. Since he is leading this rebellion, he may want to show them how harmless it is to eat of the tree. Ultimately, it does not matter. If he tasted of that fruit, it was way down on the list of his sins. We do not have these details so we will stay with what we know.

What is certain is *"He took the serpent's natural gifts and perverted them for his own nefarious purposes."*[28] *In using the serpent, it may have been kind of a you try it first. Like an expendable crewman from Star Trek, the serpent was expendable in Satan's scheme. The text does not tell us if the serpent ate of the tree. Whatever his level of participation; it was enough for God to curse him. It is not difficult to imagine a serpent being enchanted. "The practices of the snake catchers and charmers are one of the oldest Indian customs. The charmers of the most poisonous snakes in the world wear colorful turbans and devote their life to finding the perfect snake. This community leads a nomadic lifestyle and always carries dangerous and deadly snakes in their bamboo baskets. In the evening they simply sit down and start their tremendous melody, which mesmerizes the snakes. The extremely dangerous cobras are like puppies following the melody of their charmers. Although, according to the research snakescannot hear music."*[29] Apparently, it is people observing that are charmed. *"The charm has nothing to do with the music and everything to do with the charmer waving a punji, a reed instrument carved out of a gourd, in the snake's face. Snakes do not have external ears and can perceive little more than low-frequency rumbles."*[30]

---

28 Ibid. Richard.
29 http://www.thetravelerszone.com/
30 FYI: Can Snakes Really Be Charmed By Music? Ryan Bradley.

In like manner, Jannes and Jamnbres put on a show enchanting their serpents in the presence of Pharaoh and in opposition to Moses, Aaron, and their God.[31] For Satan, this is a win-win scenario. If men somehow get "one-upped" on God's people...perfect. If they fail? So what? Mankind is a bunch of inferior beings from Satan's perspective. The Hebrew word used in the case of Jannes and Jamnbres to explain the creature is the same word as in Genesis chapter 3; nachash.[32] The serpent is once again exploited in an attempt to demonstrate the enemies of God as superior to God. Pharaoh's shaman used their familiar spirits and enchantments. These sorcerers, like Eve, also bought into the content of the book, "Satan's Best Lies." Just like in the garden of Eden, Satan's plan does not work. The light-bringer failed again to bring any light. *"As Egypt was remarkably addicted to magic, sorcery, etc., it was necessary that God should permit Pharaoh's wise men to act to the utmost of their skill in order to imitate the work of God, that his superiority might be clearly seen, and his powerful working incontestably ascertained; and this was fully done when Aaron's rod swallowed up their rods."*[33] Just like in the Garden of Eden, Satan is defeated.

Satan Introduces Death To The Universe!

There is much speculation about Satan's purpose and why God allowed him into the Garden of Eden. The answer is not as complicated as the theologians have presented. Satan chose to betray all those who trusted him because he is a narcissist. He betrayed God, Adam, Eve and the creature that he used as his camouflage for his

---

31   Exodus 7:10-12
32   blueletterbible.org/lang/lexicon/lexicon.cfm?t=kjv&strongs=h5175
33   Adam Clarke Commentary. Exodus 6:12.

scheme. Satan deceived them all! This act of war brings a curse on all of them. Satan had free will. He was free to choose. He could accept that God was God or he could choose that he would be god unto himself. His repeated "I wills" in Isaiah show that he chose to defy God and declared himself to be "Most High."[34] A passage in Ezekiel gives a parallel account.[35] From this passage we receive insight about Satan. His job was reportedly an angelic guardian. Unfortunately, he became a disgruntled employee. Lucifer's beauty, wisdom and might — all the good things created in him by God — led him to pride. His pride led him to envy. His envy led to his rebellion and sin leading a global revolt against his Creator. His strategy was to enlist mankind to join him — by tempting them to succumb to the same choice that he made — to love themselves, become autonomous from God, and defy Him. The heart of the test of Adam's will was the same as Lucifer's; it was just arrayed with a different garb. They both chose to be "god" to themselves. This was, and is, the ultimate "god delusion."

Sin

We generally focus on the impact of Satan's act on mankind, but there is much more to the story. None of the participants in this debacle were created for death. They were all immortal. Satan, Adam, Eve, and any other being with access to the Tree of Life would live forever. Previous to their sinful act there was no death in the universe.[36] Sin is an action word. Their actions bring about their demise.

---

34   Why did God create a devil? Ragnar. 23/09/2012
35   Ezekiel 28:1-13
36   Romans 5:20

The Scots Confession does an excellent job of summarizing: *"We confess and acknowledge this our God to have created man (to wit, our first father Adam) to his own image and similitude, to whom he gave wisdom, lordship, justice, free will, and clear knowledge of himself; so that in the whole nature of man there could be noted no imperfection:"*[37] *from which honor and perfection man and woman did both fall; the woman being deceived by the serpent, and man obeying the voice of the woman: both conspiring against the Sovereign Majesty of God, who in expressed words had before threatened death, if they presumed to eat of the forbidden tree."*[38]

"By which transgression, commonly called Original Sin, was the image of God utterly defaced in man; and he and his posterity of nature became enemies to God, slaves to Satan, and servants to sin;[39] *insomuch that death everlasting has had, and shall have, power and dominion over all that have not been, are not, or shall not be regenerated from above: which regeneration is wrought by the power of the Holy Ghost, working in the hearts of the elect of God an assured faith in the promise of God, revealed to us in his word; by which faith we apprehend Christ Jesus, with the graces and benefits promised in him."*[40]

It is hard to grasp a time when mankind was immortal in a world where death is so much a part of our existence. Even so, it is the truth. Until Satan, Eve, Adam and their serpent friend join as co-conspirators in bringing the death penalty to mankind.[41] We

---

37 Gen. 1:26-28; Col. 3:10; Eph. 4:24
38 The Scottish Confession of Faith 1560. John Knox. Chapter 2. Gen. 3:6; 2:17
39 Ps. 51:5; Rom. 5:10; 7:5; 2 Tim. 2:26; Eph. 2:1-3
40 Ibid. Scots Confession. Chapter 3. Rom. 5:14,21 6:23; John 3:5; Rom. 5:1; Phil 1:29
41 The Heidelberg Catechism, in German, Latin and English (New York:

readily blame Satan; "the devil made me do it!" However, he did not act alone. Eve, Adam and the serpent all filled a role. We might speculate on who got the worse curse:

- Adam and Eve lose their immortality. In exchange they get pain, suffering, and physical death for their roles in Satan's war. A war against them! They participated in a war where they were the target! From this point on mankind's eternal destiny becomes uncertain.

- The ground is cursed to make things more difficult on mankind.

- Satan apparently retains some measure of immortality, but not like he previously enjoyed. His destiny is eternal fire. Satan's accomplices in the Sin of the Ages, the catalyst to Satan's war on Earth, are now his enemies, *"And I will put enmity (meaning animosity, hatred, hostility, etc.), between you and the woman, And between your seed and her Seed; He shall bruise your head, And you shall bruise His heel."*[42]

- The ill-fated serpent gets cursed to death and worse *"Because you have done this, You are cursed more than all cattle, And more than every beast of the field; On your belly you shall go, And you shall eat dust All the days of your life."*[43]

Essentially, God received Satan's declaration of war on

Charles Scribner's' Sons, 1863), 67–68. The original Latin and German verbs are redemo and erlösen.

42   Genesis 3:15 NKJV
43   Genesis 3:14 NKJV

Eve's seed as war on Earth, war on God, war on mankind, etc. He responded in a manner only God could. He pronounces judgement on all the parties involved and dispatches His armed forces to secure His Kingdom. Global peace is replaced now threatened by Satan and his angel accomplices.

Nearly all books about Satan fall into the same ploy attempting to make Satan bigger than reality. That Satan is horrible, wicked and the worst being that mankind has ever encountered is without question. Further, there is not even a close second in this contest to be the most profane. Yet, what most have written about Satan is not nearly what Scripture intended. Satan's power over us is limited. *"He cannot force us to do anything against our will. He can tempt us and fool us into doing the wrong thing. Ultimately, we have free will, and the saying 'the devil made me do it' is just flat out wrong. If Satan forced us to act against our will, then we could not be held accountable for what we did. He, therefore, can only influence us to move in a direction away from God; we have to make the choice to act in ways that contravene God's will for us. Fortunately, God has given us the antidote against Satan's poisonous ways:"*[44] Obedience and submission to God is the antidote. God asks the same thing from us that He has since the beginning — just obey.

Murder

Scripture repeatedly tells us about the character and nature of Satan. Mankind is still surprised at these accurate descriptions. Jesus minces no words. He says,

---
[44] chelmsfordcatholic.org/documents/2019/2/THE.ANSWER. IS.Feb17.2019.HowStMichaelGotHisName.pdf

CHAPTER FOUR: WHO IS SATAN?

"If God were your Father, you would love Me, for I proceeded forth and came from God; nor have I come of Myself, but He sent Me. Why do you not understand My speech? Because you are not able to listen to My Word. You are of your father the devil, and the desires of your father you want to do."[45]

Jesus accuses the Pharisees of not listening to Him. This is particularly noteworthy in the war on Earth as mankind chooses to listen to Satan rather than obey God because they prefer the voice of Satan. Jesus makes sure they understand that they are children of Satan. This is the very same charge God levels against the people of Earth in Genesis chapter 6. Mankind had become so diluted nearly everyone had become servants of Satan, even those God considered His sons. With His expectation for the sons of God in shatters, God opts to destroy the whole earth with a flood.

"Now the earth was corrupt in God's sight and was full of violence. God saw how corrupt the earth had become, for all the people on earth had corrupted their ways. So God said to Noah, "I am going to put an end to all people, for the earth is filled with violence because of them. I am surely going to destroy both them and the earth."[46]

Jesus then declares that Satan was a murderer from the beginning. Clearly, a reference to the events in the Garden of Eden in the beginning. Satan was the mastermind that caused Adam to transgress. An act that caused death to enter into the world. *This act caused the murder of Eve and all her posterity. "This was the sentiment of the Jews themselves. The wicked are called, "The children of the old serpent, who*

---

45   I John 3:4-19
46   Genesis 6:11-13

slew Adam and all his descendants."[47] Murder was on the mind of Satan when he targeted Eve. Satan deceived Eve in pursuit of bringing the demise of all mankind. Satan is the father of all mass murderers. It was through Satan that Adam transgressed, in consequence of which death entered into the world, and slew him and all his posterity.

"He who is of God hears God's words; therefore you do not hear, because you are not of God."[48]

We must all deal with the reality of inner corruption because our first parents chose the way of the one who is darkness itself. Jesus tells them that their murderous hatred of Him is rooted in their family lineage. Jesus refers to Satan's temptation of Adam and Eve in the garden, which introduced death into the experience of those who bear God's image. Since that day, all people (except Christ) have entered this world in Adam, who gave up his loving relationship with the Creator to partake of the corruption of the devil. Abandoning God as our Father, we took Satan as our father in the garden, and we have been reaping what we sowed ever since. Like those who opposed Jesus, we are born murderers, liars, and thieves, unable to please God even if we never take these evil desires to their most harmful end. Consequently, we must "become partakers of the divine nature" through faith alone in Christ.[49] Transformed from the inside out, we are enabled by the Holy Spirit to follow His law as we submit to Him."

---

47   ligonier.org/learn/devotionals/murderer-start/
48   John 8:47
49   2 Peter 1:4

CHAPTER FOUR: WHO IS SATAN?

Characteristics of Satan

The words against Lucifer by the prophet Isaiah have long been the cornerstone of our knowledge of Satan. Most scholars have interpreted this passage in a manner that gives a tremendous amount of credibility to Satan. Their interpretation lends to exactly what Satan longs for — exaltation. Attempts to paint Satan as some special exalted being are misdirected. Theologians miss the point that God has directed Isaiah to prophecy against the King of Babylon, who the prophet rightfully rails against as a minion of Satan. As the Prophet Isaiah writes a scathing rebuke about the earthly King of Babylon, Nebuchadnezzar, he is moved on by the Holy Ghost and gives prophetic insight into the character of the one that Nebuchadnezzar serves. The Prophet Isaiah (and God) saw the King Nebuchadnezzar as a sycophant of Satan and as such directed his prophetic charge against both. It is evident that the Prophet Isaiah understood that the weapons of our warfare are mighty to the pulling down of strongholds...

"... How you are fallen from Heaven, O Lucifer, son of the morning! How you are cut down to the ground, You who weakened the nations! For you have said in your heart: 'I will ascend into Heaven, I will exalt my throne above the stars of God; I will also sit on the mount of the congregation On the farthest sides of the north; I will ascend above the heights of the clouds, I will be like the Most High.'"[58]

---

58   Isaiah 14:12-17

Lucifer

Prophet Isaiah forewarns the fall of Satan from Heaven. An important point as Satan has had free reign for too long. Why God allowed Satan such liberty is debatable. In the book of Isaiah the deceiver we have referred to as Satan, the adversary, the devil, the dragon, etc. is given what seems like a proper name; Lucifer. Some claim this was his angel name. They are incorrect in this assumption. The Prophet Isaiah has not revealed Satan's proper name. Rather, like a prosecutor bringing charges, the Prophet Isaiah gives us keen insight into the character of Satan. We must keep in perspective that this is a formidable rebuke against the prince of darkness (not exaltation). He deserves nothing but what God has reserved for him.[59] Contrary to popular belief, there is no Scripture that calls Satan an archangel. The only archangel mentioned in the bible is "the Lord Himself"[60] and in reference to Jesus Christ the only one with authority to raise the dead! Mankind needs to stop exalting Satan! He has been our enemy from the beginning. He declared war on our first parents, deceived Eve and plunged all of mankind and all of the creation on earth into war, death, sickness and disease. The Prophet Isaiah references the fallen state of Lucifer and at the same time prophesied that he will be cast out of Heaven. Oh, what a wonderful prophetic word! All of the Earth can rejoice at this word of the impending termination of access to Heaven for the enemy of mankind. Isaiah's use of Lucifer is directed as an insult toward the interloper. More than an insult, this is like a cat call, "O' lucifer." "The Latin word "lucifer" as an adjective means "light-bringing."

---

[59] Jude 1:6
[60] 1 Thessalonians 4:16

CHAPTER FOUR: WHO IS SATAN?

Today the name is a synonym for the devil."[61] Theologians have postulated that Satan is the bringer of light or was at some time in the past. This is atrocious biblical exegeses. Satan has never been a bringer of light! A leopard does not change its spots![62]

Scholars have repeated this quote of Satan as the light-bringer as the angelic name of Satan. We must ask, when has Satan been a bringer of light? What light did he bring? Isn't light or being enlightened exactly what he promised Eve? Isaiah is not paying Satan compliments here but rather giving us insight into the character of Satan. Calling him "light-bringer" is indicative of his attempts to claim to be more "enlightened" than the rest of God's creation. So, light-bringer is not a compliment, it is an insult. It is a reminder and a warning to those who follow Satan's ruses in the hope that they will gain some supernatural insight, become enlightened, etc.

The proposed "light-bringer" always fails to bring light! He operates in darkness and only brings death, Hell, and destruction to his followers. As previously stated, Satan is the worst failure in the history of mankind and yet, people follow him!

Apostle Peter concurs with the Prophet Isaiah about the character of this self-aggrandizing bringer of light. "Be alert and of sober mind. Your enemy the devil prowls around like a roaring lion looking for someone to devour. Resist him, standing firm in the faith…"[63] No matter what the light-bringer brings — reject it! If

---

61   Google Dictionary
62   Jeremiah 13:23
63   1 Peter 5:8-9

Satan tries to convince you the sky is blue go outside and check! It is evident that Apostle Peter and the Prophet Isaiah both see Satan as the ruler of darkness — not a bringer of light. Apostle Paul adds: "Put on the whole armor of God, that you may be able to stand against the wiles of the devil. For we do not wrestle against flesh and blood, but against principalities, against powers, against the rulers of the darkness of this age, against spiritual hosts of wickedness in the Heavenly places."[64]

The Prophets and the Apostles agree Satan's offers of bringing light are all deceptions. To be certain that no one was confused about Satan's light bringing role, Jesus Christ spoke directly on the matter: Then Jesus spoke to them again, saying, "I am the light of the world. He who follows Me shall not walk in darkness, but have the light of life."[65] As usual, Satan merely mimics the things of God. The great pretender! We can be certain that there is room for only one bringer of light in the world. The true light-bringer actually brought light and His light is the light of the world![66]

Son of the Morning

The Prophet Isaiah rails on his adversary the devil with another insult calling him son of the morning. Isaiah links Satan's desire to be seen as a light-bringer to another of his deceptions. The Prophet indicates that the light-bringer wants to be seen as directly connected to the great light that comes up in the morning, the sun.

---

64 Ephesians 6:10-12
65 John 8:12
66 Matthew 5:14

CHAPTER FOUR: WHO IS SATAN?

Again, it seems to the casual reader like a compliment to be the son of the morning. The real deal is that the Prophet is not giving compliments. Isaiah writes that Satan is bursting with delusions. He reminds Satan that he is filled with allusions of grandeur in postulating:

- That he is responsible for the sun rising in the east.
- That he alone is the son of the morning. A great error to the multitudes of those that have or continue to worship the sun.
- That he is in control of the events of the day.

Apparently, Satan does not pretend that he created the morning. Rather, he wants mankind to accept as truth, that he is in control of the events of the day.

Somewhere we get the notion that Satan walked into the Throne room of Heaven, shook his fist at God, and declared that he would become God. That is not what happened. That is not what the Scriptures are trying to get us to understand. What happened is that Satan attacked the Kingdom of God by targeting God's special children. The only beings that are made in the image of God! Genesis 3 gives us the story. Isaiah the Prophet is scoffing at Satan's fantasies not attributing powers to him. The whole of Scripture supports this position.

WAR ON EARTH

Satan Is a Fallen Being Just Like Mankind

It is difficult to remember that Satan, Adam, and Eve were all immortal beings until they sinned in the Garden of Eden. Adam and Eve are not the only ones who fell in the Garden of Eden. All was good for Satan until iniquity was found in him.[67] The Prophet Isaiah gives us more insight into the character and nefarious accomplishments of he who would pretend to be better than mankind. He speaks of Satan's past in the Garden of Eden where he manifested as a serpent. Isaiah reminds Satan that the serpent was literally cut down to the ground. The passage is also prophetic of the coming time when Satan would lose all access to Heaven and be cast out and thrown down to Earth.[68] In witness to this prophetic word 700 years later[69] Jesus says: "*I saw Satan fall like lightning from Heaven.*"[70] Jesus is not offering this as some past experience, but rather a prophecy and confirmation of Isaiah. A prophecy not yet fulfilled, that will happen so fast and powerfully it will seem like lightning. In this same passage Jesus informs His disciples that they have power to tread on Satan![71] The curse on the serpent that Satan manipulated comes full circle as Satan finds his lofty former estate now inaccessible.

The Prophet's word is true. Satan has weakened the nations. Since Satan declared war on mankind in Genesis chapter 3 his actions have brought sin and mayhem to an earth previously filled

---

67　　Ezekiel 28:15
68　　Revelation Chapter 12
69　　https://www.biography.com/religious-figure/isaiah
70　　Luke 10:18
71　　Luke 10:19

with peace. The war that Satan brought to Earth through the sin of Genesis chapter 3 has remained a continual plague on the nations of the earth. All the nations have been weakened by his deceit.

Satan Seeks To Be Ascended

Satan's desire to ascend above the "stars of God" is the point of his obsession and his greatest delusion. He projects that he alone is the ascended master of all! The Prophet tells us that Satan has said that he will ascend into Heaven. Satan has told this lie so well and for so long that even he believes the lie. Sadly, many have fallen prey to his devices. Many who profess Christ have fallen prey to Satan's promotion of himself as an ascended being. Jesus Christ makes sure that He sets the record straight. He said that Satan has not and will not accomplish such a coup as ascending into Heaven. *"No one has ascended to Heaven but He who came down from Heaven, that is, the Son of Man."*[72]

It is noteworthy that God drives the point home "Son of Man." It might even be better understood as Son of Eve. It is a reminder of the curse in Genesis 3. Jesus Christ comes as a son of man with a mission to remind Satan that what He promised him in Genesis is coming to fruition. Lightning is about to strike! Satan's old enemy, mankind, is about to become his worst nightmare! Jesus Christ will bruise his head in ways he never imagined! This son of Eve overcomes all temptation and emerges in great victory![73] Then he passes the opportunity for "bruising the head of Satan" to them who

---

72   John 3:12-13, emp. added
73   Matthew 4:1-11

are called His sons.[74]

One of Satan's many hallucinations is that he has the power to ascend into Heaven. Satan's followers have created a whole hierarchy of pretenders who claim to be ascending. It is one of many religions of Hell.[75] We use Hell here as a word to explain the real location of Satan's headquarters.[76] There are many things that gender to Satan's little kingdom. Hell is the general catch word for Satan's malfeasance. In this version of Satan's mirage, there are three levels to becoming ascended beings.[77] The light-bringer is working his deceit. Here are his three steps:

- First, one must acquire a "spirit guide"
- Second, a "guardian angel"
- Third, then one can become an "ascended master."

Does this sound familiar? The promise of Satan that you can become like God![78] This of course is more gibberish than the serpent spewed at Eve, but mankind is often more willing to believe lies than the truth.[79] "And for this cause God shall send them strong delusion, that they should believe a lie: That they all might be damned who believed not the truth, but had pleasure in

---

[74] I John 3:1-2
[75] https://en.wikipedia.org/wiki/Hell
[76] Ezekiel 31:16
[77] The Ascended Masters: Who Are They and How Can They Help? Copyright 1995 to 2020
[78] Genesis 3:5
[79] 2 Thessalonians 2:7-12

unrighteousness."[80] It is frightening how many who claim Christ are deluded by the wiles of Satan.

Satan's hope to set his throne above the clouds so he can be like the Most High is another fantasy. It is relevant that Satan does not pretend to be God. He is only pretending to be just like God. Same promise He made Eve, "Do this and you will be like God." Being above the clouds is seen by ancient humanity as being "like God." Today, mankind routinely flies airplanes above the clouds. It is unlikely that the occupants expect this makes them like the Most High God. Though, in the days of Isaiah the Prophet, such a lofty position would give the illusion of being Godlike. The entire pantheon of gods for the Greeks and the Romans exists in such a delusion. Zeus (Jupiter) and his fellow minions live on a fantasy mountain somewhere above the proverbial clouds.[81]

A delusion likely first devised among the Canaanites who believed their pantheon of gods (originally angels of Satan) lived above the clouds of Mount Hermon.[82] Small wonder God told the children of Israel to eradicate the Canaanites. They were disciples of Satan. The exact mountain for their self-made gods was interchangeable and moved to other locations in Greece, Rome, etc. as they adopted the delusions of the Canaanites and their father, Satan. Contrary to popular myths, angels are not ascended beings and

---

80   2 Thessalonians 2:11-12
81   britannica.com/topic/Zeus
82   The Myth and Mystery of Mount Hermon. Daniel Johnson. December 15, 2019

neither is Satan. In fact, angels are now cast down to the Earth.[83]

Guardian Angels

Most people who speak of guardian angels are likely unaware of the connection of the term to Luciferian religions. These beings are not angels and they are not ascended. The Prophet Ezekiel does reference one angel as a guardian. This guardian barred Satan from the "mountain of God" likely a reference to the angel army (Cherubim) that guard the way to the Tree of Life. Being naïve does not change the facts. "Many people believe they have been assigned a specific angel in a one-on-one relationship. These specially assigned, personal protectors are called "guardian angels." Is this belief grounded in popular media, cultural desire, or biblical revelation?" Nothing in the Old or New Testament passages necessitates the existence of "guardian angels" assigned in a one-on-one relationship. There is a danger in focusing on "guardian angels." If we're not careful, we may find ourselves looking to angels for protection only God offers. When we do this, we offer angels the worship and trust due God.

Some offer that they have a guardian angel based on what some theologians have claimed. Some have even claimed to have their own spirit guide.[84] Be very careful on this slippery slope. Many people in history have fallen into this trap. Justin Martyr[85] believed

---

83   Revelation 12:7-10

84   https://myemail.constantcontact.com/A-Vision-of-William-Branham---His-Angel-Part-1.html?soid=1115977048269&aid=m6SOhMET5r8

85   The famous 2nd Century Christian apologist

CHAPTER FOUR: WHO IS SATAN?

Christians would do well to worship angels. Thomas Aquinas[86] also seemed to be quite fascinated by angels. It's important to remember angels are only described in the Bible incidental to other topics. Apostle Paul warned not to believe doctrines of demons or angels. Angels should never be the focus in and of themselves. They exist to love God and as a result, they love us. Angels are not to be the focus of our worship:[87] Let no one keep defrauding you of your prize by delighting in self-abasement and the worship of the angels…[88]

Those who are followers of Jesus Christ and those who are followers of Satan's religions find common ground in this worship of angels. Let us be succinct. There is a plethora of Scriptures to support the fact that God appoints angels to assist mankind on our journey.[89] Still, we must be careful. There are numerous Scriptures that inform us that our worship is only to God! There is not one verse encouraging mankind to worship or venerate angels. It is like Robot in the movie "Lost in Space." DANGER! DANGER! WARNING! WARNING!

People play with many things they do not understand and should leave alone. When I was about ten years old, our neighbors were playing with a Ouija board.[90] They asked me what I thought. I said, "I can tell you for certain that it's not of God." People who pray to angels, their guardian angel, saints, etc., need to realize the

---

86   Influential 13th Century Dominican theologian and philosopher
87   Does Everyone Have a Guardian Angel? J. Warner. November 25, 2019 Theology / Doctrine, Writings
88   Colossians 2:18.
89   Matthew 18:10, Psalm 91:11, 2 Kings 6:16-17
90   https://en.wikipedia.org/wiki/Ouija

only object of their prayers must be Jesus Christ. Jesus Christ holds all power in Heaven and Earth![91] This penchant toward angel veneration is based on mankind's desire to be like God! A desire exploited by Satan to the demise of all of mankind. It is a good point to remember that in Scripture when you see someone ascending it is a reference to God in some manner. Only God has control of ascension.

Stars of God

Isaiah's reference is not a reference to the physical realm as much as it is prophetic language. The stars of God are a reference to the sons of God.[92] Sons of God in Scripture are God's special children.[93] His expectation is for His sons to obey Him and do exploits in the earth.[94] When those who were sons of God failed in their responsibilities it brought great destruction to the Earth and all mankind.[95] Satan has long desired to be superior to mankind. He is obsessed with being superior to mankind even though he knows that mankind was created with superior abilities to his angel skills. To bring some relevance to his delusions Satan attempts to be seated in a place between man and God solely to frustrate the purpose of mankind. For a time, it seems that God allowed this, but Isaiah and Jesus both prophesy the demise of this access!

---

91   Mathew 28:18
92   Romans 8:14
93   Galatians 4:6
94   Daniel 11:32
95   See Genesis hapter 6

CHAPTER FOUR: WHO IS SATAN?

"It would be difficult to find anyone who, at some moment, has never looked up at the wonder of the night sky, and simply marveled at the utter beauty of the stars in breathtaking wonder. Have you ever wondered why we are ALL drawn so universally to the night skies and to their awesome beauty? The canvas of the glory of the Heavens at night is representative of the captivating nimbus of light the world is to see resting upon the church of God and within His children. For the Word declares that we, ourselves, are all called to be the stars of God. And like the stars above, it is a beautiful spectacle. The children of God are called to be a light to the world on a high hill. For what else are stars but a light in the darkness upon the hills of Heaven. We are that beauty for the world. The world is to stop and stare in wonder and amazement at the marvel of the beauty of the light in the darkness. We are to punctuate the night sky with the glory of God. And we are in the skies because we are to turn the gaze of man forever Heavenward. So that all may marvel at the wonder and glory of our Creator who abides in Heaven. Everything we see before us as the spectacle of creation is deliberate by intention and design for understanding all that which is unseen. Jesus is referred to as the 'morning star' in 2 Peter 1:19 and in Revelation 2:28. For the morning star is the brightest of all. And we are not only called to imitate Christ, but we are made in the image and likeness of our LORD. Is it any wonder, then, that we are referred to as stars? Satan desires to exalt himself ABOVE the stars of God, that is he will exalt himself in the hearts of man and get all of man to worship him." [96] As usual, Satan is fixated on his war with Eve and her descendants.[97] Legitimate sons of God [98] remain Satan's number one target.

---

96   www.warriorservants4god.org/436261247
97   Genesis 3:15
98   Hosea 1:10

Prince of Air

Daniel chapter ten shows the Prophet Daniel in a perplexed state waiting on an answer from God. God does not let him down. Uniquely, a presence shows up that is curiously described like other Biblical descriptions of Jesus Christ. While divine intervention is always the best, this particular manifestation does stand out. Satan's challenge as Prince of the Power of the Air[99] is reference to his relentless endeavors to control the space above mankind and make that arena his personal kingdom. It is not to be understood as he is in any way exalted or divine. He is the prince of naught. The reference is that he is fixated on being above mankind. Here we have yet another Prophet hurling rebuffs at the Adversary. When you give thought to it, what power is in the air? The area above the clouds is where Satan imagines that he reigns and has his imaginary throne. Those in delusion always have illusions of grandeur.

The place where Satan reigns is in an unseen realm where he seeks power over his subjects, those who give their allegiance to the enemies of God. These filthy dreamers are always imagining things. John Lennon wrote a song about illusions that he had and called it "Imagine."[100] Like Satan, John Lennon imagined that there was no Heaven and no Hell and the whole world would be one. Just like Satan's utopian dream in total defiance of God. Satan wants the whole world to imagine, as his minstrel has offered, that there is no Heaven.

---

99 Ephesians 2:2
100 https://en.wikipedia.org/wiki/Imagine_(John_Lennon_song)

CHAPTER FOUR: WHO IS SATAN?

The world was once united. That was before Satan declared war on the woman and her seed.[101] Isaiah's reference to Satan putting his throne on the mount of the congregation is yet another sham conceived in Satan's mind. This is a reference to when God spoke to the two million children of Israel from the mountain.[102] Satan schemes that he is the one who is above the mountain. In his deception if he is above the very mountain where God spoke to His people then in some part of the myth this will make him superior to mankind. He imagines that the children of Israel's veneration is for him. He will do anything to get them to worship him!

The Prophet Isaiah has added this crime to the laundry list of Satan's delusions. Not only is Satan hopeful of having his own kingdom where all of mankind is subject to his dictates, but Isaiah points out that Satan sets his kingdom at the farthest point to the north on the mountain of God. "The north" denotes those who are in ignorance. "The south," those who are "sons" and "daughters."[103] In the Book of Isaiah, the Prophet contrasts the Kingdom of God as being to the South. Thus, in pointing out Satan's desire to build his kingdom in the farthest point of the north he is using prophetic language to show us that Satan is always doing the exact extreme opposite of what God has said. Remember: Just like in Genesis 3 — Hath God said?! It is like cheese for a mouse offered in a mouse trap. Don't take the bait! It is a trap!

The Prophet Ezekiel confirms the intense warfare associated

---

101 azlyrics.com/lyrics/johnlennon/imagine.html
102 Exodus 20
103 biblemeanings.info/Words/Spatial/South.htm

with Satan's decision to sin against God. God responds to the assault on His children, Adam and Eve, as an attempt to usurp His Kingdom. The description of warfare that results is unmistakable. God dispatches his armed forces in unprecedented fashion. "The Pulpit Commentary points out: The words In the midst of the stones of fire'[104] reference God's designated power to His angelic armies. *"The cherub's sword of fire is identified with the lightning-flash, and that in its turn with the thunderbolts of God. Out of the throne of God went thunders and lightnings."*[105] The Prophet Isaiah[106] writes *"Then one of the seraphim [high-ranking angelic beings] flew to me, having in his hand a live coal which he had taken from the tongs of the altar..."* This live or "burning" coal (RSV) or, one might say, this coal of fire, was taken from the altar of God, showing the close proximity of angels to fiery coals or fiery stones."[107]

"Coals of fire or fiery stones are also used in the Bible as a reference to attributes of angels or angels themselves. In Ezekiel 10:2, 6-7, coals of fire from among the cherubim" are mentioned, and in Ezekiel 1:13, cherubim are described in this way: *"... their appearance was like burning coals of fire, like the appearance of torches going back and forth among the living creatures. The fire was bright, and out of the fire went lightning."* Revelation 4:5 describes seven angelic beings as lamps of fire burning before God's throne. Combined with the fact that especially high-ranking angelic beings such as cherubim are associated in the book of Ezekiel with or even described as "coals of fire," it is most likely that the mention of

---

104   Genesis 3:24, 2 Samuel 22:9, 15
105   Exodus 19:16
106   Isaiah 6:6
107   What are the fiery stones mentioned in Ezekiel 28:14, 16? Norbert Link. San Diego, CA.

walking in the midst of fiery stones refers to the cherub who thought himself the light-bringer (Lucifer) having a previous life where he was "walking among and having company with other cherubim and powerful angelic beings."[108] How art thou fallen from Heaven...

Mankind is more powerful than we imagine The Prophet Isaiah prophesied the end for this self-appointed light-bringer. Satan will be cast to the grave and Hell. People will be unimpressed that he is just a man. This is Isaiah chucking another in his series of verbal abuses at Satan. Realizing Satan's entire ensemble is made up of his desire to be superior to mankind; to call him a man, especially a man humiliated and disgraced, is a horrible insult. Isaiah reminds his readers of the destruction and tumult that Satan has caused throughout the world. The Prophet reminds us to be careful not to be taken in a trap by this enemy. Satan does not release his prisoners; Hell is and will continue to be populated with those who follow Satan. Satan's "kingdom" (Hell) was prepared by God for Satan and Satan's angels. The eternal fire was not created as a dwelling place of mankind.[109] Yet, men (and women) have willfully enlisted in Satan's army of those who defy God. Satan only seems to be superior to mankind because he is from another realm. When angels manifest in our realm God often empowers them to do what is impossible for mankind. One angel killed 185,000 Assyrians! Really stunning.[110] Of course this angel was the Angel of the Lord! "Consider this; what angels are capable of in our realm,

---

108   What are the fiery stones mentioned in Ezekiel 28:14, 16? Norbert Link. San Diego, CA.
109   Matthew 25:41,
110   2 Kings

mankind is capable of in their realm through the same source: Jesus Christ."[111]

Apostle Paul addressed this: *"Though we walk in the flesh — That is: Although I am in the common condition of human nature, and must live as a human being, yet I do not war after the flesh. I have a good cause, a good captain, strength at will, and courage at hand. I neither fear them nor their master. The weapons of our warfare -* [112]*Are not carnal, but mighty through God. Our doctrines are true and pure, they come from God and lead to Him, and he accompanies them with his mighty power to the hearts of those who hear them; and the strong holds — the apparently solid and cogent reasoning of the philosophers, we, by these doctrines, pull down; and thus the fortifications of heathenism are destroyed, and the cause of Christ triumphs wherever we come; and we put to flight the armies of the enemy."*[113]

Apostle Paul understood that we are at war! He speaks of the power of our weapons of warfare. "Casting down imaginations, reasonings, or opinions."[114] The same methods used by Satan in Genesis and throughout history. *"The Greek philosophers valued themselves especially on their ethic systems, in which their reasonings appeared to be very profound and conclusive; but they were obliged to assume principles which were either such as did not exist, or were false in themselves, as the whole of their mythologic system most evidently was: truly, from what remains of them we see that their metaphysics were generally bombast; and as to their philosophy, it was*

---

111   Interview with Bernie L. Wade, II. Life Church of Kentucky. December 4, 2020.

112   Ephesians 6:10-17; 1 Timothy 1:18; 2 Timothy 2:3-5

113   Adam Clarke Commentary. 2 Chronicles 10

114   Adam Clarke 2 Chronicles Chapter 10

CHAPTER FOUR: WHO IS SATAN?

in general good for nothing. When the apostles came against the gods many and their lords many with the One Supreme and Eternal Being, they were confounded, scattered, annihilated; when they came against their various modes of purifying the mind — their sacrificial and mediatorial system, with the Lord Jesus Christ, his agony and bloody sweat, his cross and passion, his death and burial, and his glorious resurrection and ascension, they sunk before them, and appeared to be what they really were, as dust upon the balance, and lighter than vanity."[115]

"The knowledge of God - The doctrine of the unity and eternity of the divine nature, which was opposed by the plurality of their idols, and the generation of their gods, and their men-made deities. It is amazing how feeble a resistance heathenism made, by argument or reasoning, against the doctrine of the Gospel! It instantly shrunk from the Divine light and called on the secular power to contend for it! The apostles destroyed heathenism wherever they came; the Protestants confuted popery wherever their voice was permitted to be heard." Satan is defeated!

"Bringing into captivity every thought - Heathenism could not recover itself; in vain did its thousands of altars smoke with reiterated hecatombs, their demons were silent, and their idols were proved to be nothing in the world. Popery could never, by any power of self-reviviscence, restore itself after its defeat by the Reformation: it had no Scripture, consecutively understood; no reason, no argument; in vain were its bells rung, its candles lighted, its auto dafe's exhibited; in vain did its fires blaze; and in vain were innumerable human victims immolated on its altars!"[116]

"The obedience of Christ - Subjection to idols was annihilated by the

---

115   Adam Clarke 2 Chronicles Chapter 10.
116   Ibid. Clarke.

progress of the Gospel among the heathens; and they soon had but one Lord, and his name one. In like manner the doctrines of the reformation, mighty through God, pulled down - demolished and brought into captivity, the whole papal system; and instead of obedience to the pope, the pretended vicar of God upon earth, obedience to Christ, as the sole almighty Head of the Church, was established, particularly in Great Britain, where it continues to prevail. Hallelujah! The Lord God Omnipotent reigneth!"[117]

All the Terms in These Verses Are Military

Theologians are surprised at the military bearing of Scripture. It is evident that the writers (or the Holy Spirit moving through the writers) realized this is war! Apostle Paul *"Mentions a strongly fortified city, where the enemy had made his last stand; entrenching himself about the walls; strengthening all his redoubts and ramparts; raising castles, towers, and various engines of defense and offense upon the walls; and neglecting nothing that might tend to render his strong hold impregnable. The army of God comes against the place and attacks it; the strong holds, all the fortified places, are carried. The imaginations, engines, and whatever the imagination or skill of man could raise, are speedily taken and destroyed. Every high thing, all the castles and towers are sapped, thrown down and demolished; the walls are battered into breaches; and the besieging army, carrying everything at the point of the sword, enter the city, storm and take the citadel. Everywhere defeated, the conquered submit, and are brought into captivity, are led away captives; and thus, the whole government is destroyed."*[118] Apostle Paul finishes his instruction by reminding us who we are in Christ Jesus! *"I have a greater authority and spiritual power*

---

117 Ibid. Clarke.
118 Ibid. Clarke.

than I have yet shown, both to edify and to punish;"[119]

Justice and Mercy

God always dispenses justice with mercy. Justice requires mercy. Without mercy, justice is too overbearing. Without justice, mercy is too lascivious. While God curses Satan (Adam, Eve, and the serpent), He also provides hope and a prophecy of the future for the posterity of Adam and Eve.

It is particularly pointed to the woman so as to give her hope that in spite of the horrible consequences of her action, redemption will come! *"... the seed of the woman should break down the serpent's head*[120] *- that is, he should destroy the works of the devil. Which promise, as it was repeated and made clearer from time to time, so was it embraced with joy, and most constantly received of all the faithful, from Adam to Noah, from Noah to Abraham, from Abraham to David, and so forth to the incarnation of Christ Jesus: all (we mean the faithful fathers) under the law did see the joyful days of Christ Jesus, and did rejoice."*[121]

The president of a Presbyterian seminary argued that it was simply impossible to preach the Christian gospel with full force and joy apart from a frank admission that, in the "biblical view of the human situation," we are oppressively enslaved by the powers of sin, death and, indeed, the evil.[122] The *"doctrine of a personal power*

---

119 Ibid. Clarke.
120 Gen. 3:15
121 Ibid. Scots Confession. Chapter 4.
122 Donald G. Miller, "Preaching the Gospel," Essays Presented to Markus

of evil is of the utmost importance to dogmatics as a foundation of the true doctrine of sin and redemption."[123]

In the Garden of Eden, mankind gave up his immortality to follow the advice of Satan. In Christ Jesus, God robes Himself in flesh, comes to the earth, and creates a path for redemption of His most favored creation. The path for mankind to find their way back to immortality is through the death, burial, and resurrection of Jesus Christ.

Barth on His Sixty-fifth Birthday, edited by Dikran Y. Hadidian (Pittsburgh: Pittsburgh Theological Monographs, 1981), 205–226, especially 211–19.

123   John MacPherson, Christian Dogmatics (Edinburgh: T&T Clark, 1898), 220. See Gen. 12:3; 15:5-6; 2 Sam. 7:14; Isa. 7:14; 9:6; Hag. 2:6; John 8:56

Chapter 5
Two Trees in the Garden

"Sorrow is knowledge: they who know the most must mourn the deepest o'er the fatal truth, the Tree of Knowledge is not that of Life."

—George Gordon Byron, Manfred

Central to the whole of the story of Satan declaring war on God through his sin in the Garden is the Tree of Life. The appearance of the cherubim in the Garden of God should not be a surprise. A battle involving immortal beings is in process. God manifests His might! Here in the Garden was the Tree of Life. The Tree of Life is a manifestation of Jesus Christ. The presence of this particular "tree" indicates that not only did Adam and Eve love the Garden, but also that God used it as a dwelling place or at least a very special place.

There is nothing like the Garden of Eden in the whole of creation. It is not a small thing that God plants the Garden and then places first His son Adam and then Eve. When we see the Tree of Life as a manifestation of God, we understand that God was in the Garden of Eden. When we look closer that God "walked through the Garden in the cool of the evenings" we begin to see a picture of the breath of God moving through His Garden and all of His creation responding. This includes His special children Adam and Eve. Sadly, all of this beauty is destroyed by man's sinfulness.

Satan's First Assault

In every conflict there is an initial phase. We might call this the first assault. This battle generally sets the tone for the rest of the War. The assault on Eden by Satan and his allies is not a small matter. This action is the first salvo in this war. In fact, it is the pivotal point in the history of mankind. *"For a time, Lucifer hid his true plans under a 'mask' of love and respect for God. Lucifer pretended to honor God. But he was really trying to cause angels to feel unhappy with God's laws."*[1]

It seems that at the same time he was currying favor with the angel kind. Satan was also busy working a similar ploy on mankind. While Satan has no more power than the others, he does emerge as their leader.

---

1   Ellen G. White, The Great [big] Controversy [war between God and Satan], page 495; adapted.

CHAPTER FIVE: TWO TREES IN THE GARDEN

"The world has rushed to embrace the fictitious Darth Vader while generally ignoring the very real Satan."

All that happens throughout recorded history is impacted from this incident. God would not simply ignore Satan. This was not a slight breach. This was a full-scale offensive. The problem is that many people do not believe there is a war on Earth, because they do not believe in Satan. Sadly, this group of people includes some Christians. What do they think about Bible verses that talk about Satan, or the devil? These people say that the devil is just a word picture the Bible uses to explain evil and suffering. These individuals don't really believe the Bible means the devil is real. To deny the existence of the enemy of God is an allied position to denying God.[2] For many people, the idea of a powerful and evil angel who wants to destroy humans is only a made-up story, the same as Darth Vader from the movie Star Wars is made up."[3] Ironically, Vader is a German word meaning "father."

The world has rushed to embrace the fictitious Darth Vader while generally ignoring the very real Satan. While we are quick to place all the blame on Satan, we should focus on Scripture. Here we learn that Adam and not Satan brought sin to us.

> "For if when we were enemies we were reconciled to God through the death of His Son, much more, having been reconciled, we shall be saved by His life. And not only that, but we also rejoice in God through our Lord Jesus

---

2   Quote from 1992. Bernie L. Wade.
3   SATAN'S LIES AND TRICKS IN THE LAST DAYS. Easy Reading Edition.

Christ, through whom we have now received the reconciliation." [4]

Satan sinned, to be sure. However, Satan is not mankind. He induced mankind to sin but Satan's sin is against God. We could liken this to an adult inducing a child to take a gun and rob a bank. To be sure both the person planning the heist and the child are bank robbers but the law will hold a different view of the severity of each of their transgressions. In like manner, Satan is dealt with by God in a different manner than Adam and Eve.

The Plan Was Diabolical

The Spanish word Diablo comes from the Latin, and in both languages means, the devil as the personification of evil. It is uniquely associated with the English word diabolical[5] which means extremely evil and is a characteristic of Satan (the devil). In Daniel chapter 6, we find an interesting parallel to the diabolical plan of Satan. We learn of a law; a particular law of the Medes and Persians during Israel's time in exile. According to this law, any laws or proclamations that are made cannot be altered. This means once it is written, the law stands.

"The law basically made the king powerless to help his friend. Though, that was probably the point of the law against repealing laws; it was likely used to limit the kings' whims and favoritism. So, although extremely inconvenient, it seemed to serve a good purpose."[6] In the Daniel account, the law is used as

---

4 Romans 5:10-11
5 Dictionary.com Diabolical.
6 The Layman's Bible. The Inconvenient Law of the Medes and Persians.

a scheme. First, some of the kingdom's officials conspire to get the king to pass a law to be in effect for 30 days. Then, they use the law to bring accusation against Daniel. The penalty is death. The king is extremely upset that he has in effect been duped but his hands are tied. It is the law. A similar event takes place in the time of Queen Esther.

"There is a certain people dispersed and scattered among the peoples in all the provinces of your kingdom whose customs are different from those of all other people and who do not obey the king's laws; it is not in the king's best interest to tolerate them. If it pleases the king, let a decree be issued to destroy them, and I will put ten thousand talents of silver into the royal treasury for the men who carry out this business." [7]

In a similar scheme to those used on Daniel and Esther, Satan seeks to find a horrible egregious act that is unalterable in the law of God. He determines that by conning God's new woman, Eve, into eating of the Tree of Knowledge mankind will be condemned. Satan assumes this will make him superior to mankind. The penalty is death. The law of God is straightforward. Partake of this tree and you will die. Satan convinced Eve that if she eats of the tree she will not die. It is a lie, but he doesn't care. Eve's dilemma was to choose between the Word of God or the voice of Satan. Satan definitely knows God will keep His word. Satan takes advantage of God's immutability.

November 28, 2015.
7   Esther 3:8-9

Satan knows that "God is not a man, that He should lie, nor a son of man, that He should change His mind. Does He speak and then not act? Does He promise and not fulfill?" No, God does not change His mind. He is unchanging and unchangeable. He said if they eat of the tree, they will die and it happened.[8] They ate the tree, they had to die.

Death in Adam, Life in Christ

"The death of Adam and Eve was both literal and spiritual. Adam's spiritual death was immediate even though his physical death would be much later. "Adam walked with God in the cool of the day. The Hebraic rendering of the word cool is ruwach breath or Spirit. Adam walked with God in the Spirit or breath of the day; this is seemingly equivalent to what covenant believers experience in the Holy Ghost today. The pain of judgment immediately terminated the spiritual intimacy that Adam enjoyed with God the day he partook of the forbidden fruit. As a result, God disenfranchised Adam and his posterity from covenantal intimacy by driving them from His presence. Thus, Adam ceased to live before his God. Sin permanently shattered that relationship when disobedience induced the rendering of his judgment." [9]

"But you are not in the flesh but in the Spirit, if indeed the Spirit of God dwells in you. Now if anyone does not have the Spirit of Christ, he is not His. And if Christ is in you, the body is dead because of sin, but the Spirit is life because of righteousness."[10]

8	Number 23:19
9	The Death of Adam. Febus. Page 2
10	Romans 8:9-10

CHAPTER FIVE: TWO TREES IN THE GARDEN

"Therefore, just as through one man sin entered the world, and death through sin, and thus death spread to all men, because all sinned — For until the law sin was in the world, but sin is not imputed when there is no law. Nevertheless, death reigned from Adam to Moses, even over those who had not sinned according to the likeness of the transgression of Adam, who is a type of Him who was to come."[11] Apostle Paul confirms that Adam brought sin to all mankind. He does not blame Eve, as modern preachers are apt because of cultural influences. The Apostle points out that mankind became the enemies of God. Certainly, this does not excuse Satan's resulting war on Earth but rather places the severity of the sin on Adam. Adam did not have to listen to the voice of his wife. Adam should have obeyed the Word of God. Satan has no capacity to force his confusion on mankind. Only Adam is the ancestor of mankind. Satan has no part in the regeneration of mankind. Thus, the sin brought to mankind is from Adam. Death brought upon mankind is from Adam. According to the law and order of God, only a son of Adam may bring the redemption to mankind. Thus, a dilemma. Where is a man who is sinless and would sacrifice himself for the redemption of mankind?

Christ chose Mary as a conduit to redeem mankind. Mary was a variable. God could have chosen any qualified woman. Mary met His criteria. Christ being born of a woman made Him not only God but also a Son of Man. The redemption plan for the sons of God was paramount to the mission of Christ. Apostle Paul speaks directly to the charges brought against mankind in Genesis 6. Here God speaks of His displeasure with those who are sons of God continuing in the

---

11   Romans 5:12-14

pattern of sin brought by Adam. Apostle Paul reminds us that those who did not sin, like Adam sinned, were subject to death brought by Adam, but their lives not stained by sin are like unto Jesus Christ. The Apostle does not name these saints, but it is a reference to those in Hebrews chapter 11 and other similar references.

The Tree Of Life

"In the book of Genesis, God places the Tree of Life and the Tree of Knowledge of Good and Evil in the middle of the Garden of Eden where the tree of life stands as a symbol of God's life-giving presence and the fullness of eternal life vailable in God."[12] The Garden of Eden, perhaps more fittingly referred to as the Garden of God, *"...was apparently the dwelling-place of God. In the polytheistic story of the creation of the world and early life of man, which, while in several respects analogous,[13] the garden was the abode of the gods who alone had access to the Tree of Life from the fruit of which they derived their immortality."[14]* The Tree of Life is presented as the life source for Adam and Eve. In the Genesis account, we learn that in spite of the numerous trees in "Creation" creation there are only two substantial ones in the Garden of Eden. *"The Tree of Life is mentioned in the Bible in the Book of Genesis. It is the tree that grows within the Garden of Eden and is the source of eternal life. The tree has healing properties and its fruit grants immortality."* The connection of the Tree of Life to immortality helps us to understand why Adam and Eve who had fallen from immortality due to their willfulness to ignore

---

12 What Is the Tree of Life in the Bible? - Learn Religions www.learnreligions.com › Christianity › The Bible

13 compare Genesis 3:22

14 biblestudytools.com/dictionary/cherubim-1/

the commandments of God, were barred access back to the Tree of Life. Too much emphasis is placed on the Tree of Knowledge of Good and Evil and not enough on the Tree of Life.

"In Eden, the tree appears to have been a source of ongoing physical life. The presence of the tree of life suggests a supernatural provision of life as Adam and Eve ate the fruit their Creator provided. Adam and Eve were designed to live forever, but to do so they likely needed to eat from the tree of life. Once they sinned, they were banned from the Garden, separated from the tree, and subject to physical death, just as they had experienced spiritual death. Since Eden, death has reigned throughout history."[15]

We are introduced to the Tree of the Knowledge of Good and Evil for the very first time in Genesis 2:9, *"And out of the ground the Lord God caused to grow every tree that is pleasing to the sight and good for food; the Tree Of Life also in the midst of the garden, and the Tree Of The Knowledge Of Good And Evil."*

"There are only two trees which are named among all the trees here in the garden — the Tree of Life and the Tree of The Knowledge Of Good and Evil. Both trees are in the midst of the garden, displayed prominently, easily accessible to Adam and Eve. One tree was the Tree of Life. The other tree was the Tree of Death. Of course, it was not called the Tree of Death, but it was that and more."[16] If this tree did not hold some mystery then there would be no temptation to eat of it, and no real test of submission and obedience to God. "The name 'The

---

15   What is the Tree of Life? Randy Alcorn. Eternal Perspective Ministries. 2016 24 Oct.
16   Christ – The Tree of Life. Brian Anderson. April 21st, 2013 | by Brian Anderson

Tree of the Knowledge of Good and Evil' was actually a very accurate description. By eating of the tree man would know the good he had forfeited and the evil which he had plunged into."[17]

"The next time the Tree of The Knowledge of Good and Evil occurs is in Genesis 2:16-17, 'And the Lord God commanded the man, saying, From any tree of the garden you may eat freely; but from the Tree of the Knowledge of Good and Evil you shall not eat, for in the day that you eat from it you shall surely die.' God allowed man free reign to eat of any tree in the garden, including the Tree of Life, except for the Tree of the Knowledge of Good and Evil. As long as Adam and Eve obeyed God's one and only law, they would live in continual fellowship with God. If they had never eaten from the Tree of the Knowledge of Good and Evil they would still be alive today! The choice for Adam and Eve was straightforward the Tree of Life is for eternal life. The forbidden tree brings death."[18]

"If Adam and Eve refused to eat from this tree, it would mean that they would need to be in constant dependence upon God. God has the knowledge of good and evil. They didn't. Thus, they would need to look to God to tell them what was good and what was evil, what was right and what was wrong. By partaking of this fruit, they would become independent of God. In a very real sense, every member of the human race has eaten of the Tree of the Knowledge of Good and Evil. When you and I live independently of God, it proves that in a real sense, we have done exactly what Adam and Eve did in the garden. When we make decisions without consulting God, and go our own way, it proves we have eaten from the forbidden tree. All of us like sheep have gone astray, each of us has turned to his own way."[19]

---

17   Ibid. Anderson.
18   Ibid. Anderson.
19   Ibid. Anderson. See Is. 53:6

The Tree of Life is more than a tree. *"If the Tree of the Knowledge of Good and Evil points us to sin, the curse, death, and alienation, what does the Tree of Life point us to?"*

- Righteousness: *"Blessed are those who wash their robes, that they may have the right to the Tree of Life and may enter by the gates into the city."*[20] Interestingly, the first tree has to do with sin, but the second tree has to do with righteousness. Those who eat from the Tree of Life are those who have washed their robes. *"They have washed their robes and made them white in the blood of the Lamb."*[21] The blood of Jesus Christ cleanses us from all sin. To wash our robes is symbolic of a complete and total cleansing of our lives from every stain and blemish of sin.

- Healing: *"And he showed me a river of the water of life, clear as crystal, coming from the throne of God and of the Lamb, in the middle of its street. And on either side of the river was the Tree of Life, bearing twelve kinds of fruit, yielding its fruit every month; and the leaves of the tree were for the healing of the nations. And there shall no longer be any curse."*[22] The Tree of the Knowledge of Good and Evil brought forth the curse. The Tree of Life brings forth the blessing and healing. In Christ, there is no longer any curse. Sin has ravaged mankind. All of us are broken people because of sin. Our intellect, emotions, and will are all wrong. We think wrongly, feel wrongly, and choose wrongly. We need healing; this is exactly what God does for us through the Tree of Life.

20	Revelation 22:14
21	Revelation 7:14
22	Revelation 22:1-3

He restores us to perfect health, physically, intellectually, emotionally, and volitionally. We are sinners, sorry and wrecked by the Fall. We may use the leaves from the Tree of Life for our ultimate and perfect healing.

- Life: We ought to know that this tree would bring forth life, because it is called the Tree of Life! Just as the first tree brought spiritual and eternal life. Those who partake of the Tree of Life "they shall reign forever and ever."[23] Everlasting life in the presence of God and of the Lamb is the portion for those who partake of this tree.

- Reconciliation: By eating of the first tree, Paradise was lost. By eating of the Tree of Life, Paradise is restored. *"And there shall no longer be any curse; and the throne of God and of the Lamb shall be in it, and His bond-servants shall serve Him; and they shall see His face, and His name shall be on their foreheads."*[24] Instead of being turned out of Paradise, we are brought back into Paradise. Instead of being banished from the immediate presence of God, we see His face. Instead of alienation, we find reconciliation. His name is on our foreheads. I am my beloved's and He is mine.

Where Is The Tree Of Life?

"To him who overcomes, I will grant to eat of the tree of life, which is in the Paradise of God."[25] The Tree of Life is in the Paradise of God. It is obviously in a realm where access is not granted to fallen mankind.

---

23 Revelation 22:5
24 Revelation 22:3-4
25 Revelation 2:7

CHAPTER FIVE: TWO TREES IN THE GARDEN

It is in same place as the Garden of Eden. We know that the Holy Spirit is that Gift! *"For whatever is born of God overcomes the world; and this is the victory that has overcome the world — our faith. And who is the one who overcomes the world, but he who believes that Jesus is the Son of God?"*[26] Who is the overcomer? The one who believes in Jesus Christ. The Tree of Life is given as a gift to believers in Christ, those who overcome by faith. Apostle John also tells us, *"the leaves of the tree are for the healing of the nations."*[27] Nations will be healed by the Tree of Life. Since we will not experience pain or disease in Heaven, it is evident that this is for us now! "Our physical life and health, even our healing, comes not from our intrinsic immortal nature but from partaking of God's gracious provision in the fruit and leaves of the Tree of Life. Hence, our well- being is not granted once for all but will be forever sustained and renewed as we depend on Him and draw from His provision."[28] This is just as it was for Adam and Eve in the Garden of Eden.

It seems evident that Jesus Christ came to restore what was lost. What is it that man lost? Immortality! Man, who was immortal, lost his immortality when he ate of the forbidden tree. God robed Himself in flesh and brought restoration — a path to the Tree of Life. The fulfillment of His promise to Eve has come. Satan is truly crushed under the heel of Jesus Christ. The key to immortality is the Tree of Life, Jesus Christ.

> *"And so it is written, The first man Adam was made a living soul; the last Adam was made a quickening spirit. Howbeit that was not first which is*

---

26 1 John. 5:4-5
27 Revelation 22:2
28 Ibid. Alcorn.

spiritual, but that which is natural; and afterward that which is spiritual. The first man is of the earth, earthy; the second man is the Lord from Heaven. As is the earthy, such are they also that are earthy: and as is the Heavenly, such are they also that are Heavenly. And as we have borne the image of the earthy, we shall also bear the image of the Heavenly. Now this I say, brethren, that flesh and blood cannot inherit the kingdom of God; neither doth corruption inherit incorruption. Behold, I shew you a mystery; We shall not all sleep, but we shall all be changed, In a moment, in the twinkling of an eye, at the last trump: for the trumpet shall sound, and the dead shall be raised incorruptible, and we shall be changed. For this corruptible must put on incorruption, and this mortal must put on immortality. So when this corruptible shall have put on incorruption, and this mortal shall have put on immortality, then shall be brought to pass the saying that is written, Death is swallowed up in victory. O death, where is thy sting? O grave, where is thy victory? The sting of death is sin; and the strength of sin is the law. But thanks be to God, which giveth us the victory through our Lord Jesus Christ. Therefore, my beloved brethren, be ye steadfast, unmovable, always abounding in the work of the Lord, forasmuch as ye know that your labor is not in vain in the Lord."[29]

---

29   I Corinthians 15:45-54

Chapter 6
Angels

"I marvel that you are turning away so soon from Him who called you in the grace of Christ, to a different gospel, which is not another; but there are some who trouble you and want to pervert the gospel of Christ. But even if we, or an angel from Heaven, preach any other gospel to you than what we have preached to you, let him be accursed." [1]

So, let us have a discussion about angels. It is undeniable that mankind has a fascination with angels. It is partly because angels are from a realm beyond that of mankind. Some refer to this as supernatural. However, this writer contends that there is only the realm of God and the realm of men. If there is truly a supernatural realm, then it is the realm of God. Attempts to use alternate means to reach God are referred to as supernatural but they are really the domain of Satan.[2] Those who delve into this false realm receive chaos, disease, death, and every evil work.

---

1   Galatians 1:6-9
2   John 10:1

Another rationale for the fascination with angels, is angels are immortal beings. Immortality is what Adam and Eve traded for a taste of the fruit from the Tree of the Knowledge of Good and Evil. Horrible trade to be certain. Contrary to what people first think, other than Satan, angels did not interact with the affairs of men until the time of Abraham. Before this, the only reference we have of angels is Satan's interference with God's perfect order and the cherubim who manifested their presence in Eden as a part of God's response to Satan's skullduggery. Also, there is reference to the Angel of the Lord which is undoubtedly a manifestation of God.

Angels interacting with man first appear in Scripture in relation to Abraham and Lot. God meets Abram. He has two others with him.[3] Later we learn that these other two are the angels[4] that go to Sodom to rescue Lot.[5] These two unnamed angels are serious business. These angels are so repulsed by the activity in Sodom that they don't even want to be indoors inside the city. *"And they said unto him, for we lodge in the street. Knowing the disposition of the inhabitants of Sodom, and appearing in the mere character of travelers, they preferred the open street to any house; but as Lot pressed them vehemently, and they knew him to be a righteous man, not yet willing to make themselves known, they consented to take shelter under his hospitable roof."*[6] The men of Sodom are so debased they thought they could have homosexual relations with angels! The inhabitants of Sodom are without proper spiritual training or they would have

---

[3] Genesis 18

[4] Genesis 18. Introduction. https://www.studylight.org/commentaries/acc/genesis-19.html

[5] Genesis 19

[6] Adam Clarke Commentary. Genesis 18:2

known that angels do not have physical bodies.[7] What they were seeing is only a manifestation. The angels were not playing games. They smote these horrible men with blindness. The next day, the entire city is destroyed with fire and brimstone.

"I really don't know where the idea came from that deserving humans were upgraded to angel status in Heaven, but it is seriously misdirected. That is neither a compliment to angels nor humans. Angels and humans are both created by God for different purposes. Angels have personalities, but they are not persons. They were created by God, but not in His image. Angels are not only different from humans, but they are also different from each other. Some are 'cherubim' while others are 'seraphim.' Each has his own mind,[8] will,[9] and emotions.[10] They don't appear to mankind to look alike. Some have wings and some appear to us just like humans." [11/12]

Angels Were Created

Angels were created to serve mankind.[13] They were not created with the goal being for them to evolve into mankind. It is an oft presented notion by writers of fiction, but not true in the realm of God. Scripture refers to angels as "servants."[14] They are not

---

7   Ephesians 6:12
8   2 Samuel 14:20
9   Revelation 22:8-9
10 Hebrews 12:22
11 Isa 6, Ex 3
12 The Truth About Angels in the Bible. Candida Moss. Jul. 11, 2017 9:07PM ET. Aug. 15, 2013 4:45AM ET.
13 Psalm 103:20
14 Hebrews 1:7

only God's servants, but also our servants: *"Are they not all ministering spirits sent out to serve those who are going to inherit salvation?"*[15]

This Scripture makes it very clear that the job of angels is to serve mankind, but not all mankind. Rather, a specific group. Those who are sons of God, those who are heirs of salvation! This is exactly what caused the rebellion of Satan and his angels in Eden so many millennia ago. They were not willing to serve mankind — especially those who would become the sons of God. When God's people ran out of food in the desert, God gave them manna. Some refer to manna as "the bread of angels".[16] Angels also ministered to Elijah with food and drink after he ran for his life from Jezebel in the desert all day.[17] Jesus got the same V.I.P. treatment after His 40 days in the desert. Noticeably, all these incidents involved God's angels.

The Scripture only speaks of God's angels and Satan's angels. It seems that no one else holds any claims on angels. "The literal term 'fallen angel' appears neither in the Bible nor in other Abrahamic Scriptures but is used to describe angels who were cast out of Heaven or angels who sinned. Such angels often tempt humans to sin."[18] The major reason that these angels are not called fallen angels in Scripture is because they were not cast out of Heaven until the events at Calvary. In the beginning angels were terribly frightening creatures that were prepared for war. There is no reason to believe that has

---

15   Hebrews 1:14
16   Psalm 78:25
17   1 Kings 19:6
18   Fallen angel - Wikipediaen.wikipedia.org › wiki › Fallen angel

changed. While we do not know at what point God felt the need for angels to do warfare, it is evident that angels are most often used in some capacity of warfare. We first witness this in the text of the book of Genesis when God's cherubim manifest in defense of Eden. This is apparently to defend the Tree of Life which is in the Garden of God (Garden of Eden). Various passages throughout Scripture add to our understanding of this realm. What starts out as something completely composed of another realm is over time re-imagined by mankind as something less terrible. *"In the fifteen hundred years since the Bible was put together, angels have been made over into the shoulder-length-haired, blue-eyed, white robed Caucasians that adorn laminated prayer cards."*[19] Resonances are good, but these are not the angels of the Bible. These are the illusions of men. The angels of the Bible are quite different. *"Seraphim are large six-winged snakes that fly. Cherubs aren't well-fed babies, they're winged lions."*[20]

Satan emerged in the Garden of God to Eve. How he did this is much less important than what he caused to happen. Satan is an angel. Angel is his kind or species. Sin did not cause him to change species. He remains an angel. Angels sometimes manifest in our realm, but this is not their natural habitation. Angels were created before the genesis of mankind. This was before Satan's rebellion against the plan of God and the simultaneous war on mankind that causes war on Earth. The entire cosmos is impacted by this action. The alliance of some angels with Satan brings the realm of angels into warfare with mankind. Mankind is the children of God,

---

19   The Truth About Angels in the Bible. Candida Moss. Jul. 11, 2017 9:07PM ET. Aug. 15, 2013 4:45AM ET.

20   Ibid. Moss.

this assault on His children results in war. This is the reason God responds in Genesis with manifesting His cherubim. It also explains why mankind is challenged and warned to be wary when it comes to angels, and those who claim to have spoken to an angel. It is an angel that started all of mankind's struggles.

Apostle Paul is very forceful when it comes to what mankind is to accept from angels. Apostle Paul curses those who would follow doctrines of angels which he labels doctrines of demons. Apostle Paul is in good standing in so doing. God had already cursed those who welcome doctrines of demons. Apostle Paul's admonitions are just reminders of the divine imprimatur. Eve's willingness to listen to an angel, heed the instruction of an angel, and act on that instruction cost her immortality! Not to by any means be degrading to angels, but "in the Bible angels are mostly errand boys, the word itself means 'messenger.'[21] As God's intermediaries they give tours of Heaven to righteous visionaries like Daniel, deliver messages to God's chosen ones, and praises to God. There are many kinds of angels, from the familiar (the angels, archangels, cherubs) to the strangely inanimate."[22]

Armed Forces

Angels have a violent streak. "The first angels mentioned in the Bible are the cherubim that guard the Tree of Life in the Garden of Eden. Each of these squadron of angels is armed with a

---

21   Google Dictionary. Angel. Religion.
22   The Truth About Angels in the Bible. Candida Moss. Jul. 11, 2017 9:07PM ET. Aug. 15, 2013 4:45AM ET.

fiery ever-turning sword. The dispatching of God's armed cherubim is the first indicator that war was declared on Earth. The Eden story is not an isolated affair. The Angel of the Lord is always packing heat. More often than not, if an angel shows up to an event in the Hebrew Bible, it is to harm someone.[23]

Angels are God's Messengers, not musicians. *"Biblical angels (Heb, malakhim) may be defined as nondivine, Heavenly messengers whose function it is to relay divine information, accompany God when He appears before humans, and assist or punish humans on God's behalf."*[24] One of only two angels mentioned by name is Gabriel. The other is Michael who we learn is a theophany of Jesus Christ. Gabriel presents as God's primary sentinel or messenger. "In Luke 1, we see Gabriel bringing important and good news to both Zachariah and Mary."

We never see Gabriel sing. We never see any angels sing in the Bible. Singing and playing harps? No! Praising God? Yes! *"A multitude of the Heavenly host was praising God and saying: 'Glory to God in the highest, and on earth peace, good will toward men.'"*[25] The word peace is notable as it leaves the impression that the Earth must have been without peace previous to the arrival of Jesus Christ. "Of all the Scriptures about angels, not one time are they singing or playing an instrument (the shofar/trumpet is often used for military purposes). You may wonder — why not? Maybe singing is our job? God created

---

23   The Truth About Angels in the Bible. Candida Moss. Jul. 11, 2017 9:07PM ET. Aug. 15, 2013 4:45AM ET.

24   Gabriel Blow Your Horn! - A Short History of Gabriel within Jewish Literature. David L. Everson Classics Department. Xavier University (Cincinnati, OH). December 2009

25   Luke 2:13

His image-bearers with the capacity to worship and I wonder if angels are shaking their heads when they see us watching instead of worshiping on Sundays.[26]

God's Imperial Army

When God's cherubim arrive on the scene, it is a serious matter. *"On one occasion, during the reign of King David, when the Angel of the Lord is about to destroy Jerusalem, God has to tell him to put his sword away.[27] Warfare is certainly one of the job descriptions of angels. No wonder God deploys His cherubim in response to Satan's mutiny in the Garden. Biblically speaking, angels are as likely to be sending a message as delivering one."[28]* If you are looking for spiritual assistance, call on God or a minister of God. If you meet an angel, you should probably run if you can! If not, fall on your face!

God Created Angels

Angels have not always existed. According to Scripture, they are a part of the universe God created. In a passage that refers to angels (the "host" or "armies" of Heaven), we read, *"You are the Lord, you alone; you have made Heaven, the Heaven of Heavens, with all their host...and the host of Heaven worships you."[29]* In the New Testament, Paul tells us that God created all things "visible and invisible," and specifically includes the angelic world with the phrase "whether

---
26   GOD'S ANGEL ARMY. Mark Dance. December 22, 014 298
27   thedailybeast.com/the-truth-about-angels-in-the-bible
28   Ibid. Moss.
29   Nehemiah 9:6

thrones or dominions or principalities or authorities."[30] The author of Hebrews advocates that all angels are "spirits." When Jesus appears to the disciples, He asserts that "spirits" do not have a body like He does.[31] Thus, angels are very unlike mankind. In the Bible, angels cannot usually be seen by humans unless God reveals them.[32] From time to time with the imprimatur of Almighty God, angels took on a form to appear similar to mankind to appear to various people in Scripture.[33] These actions are about God making sure His message is received in a manner that does not freak out His children.

Cherubim - Angel Armies

Cherubim are mentioned in several places throughout Scripture:

They guarded the entrance to the Eden (Genesis 3:24)

God is enthroned above them (Ezekiel 10:1–22)

God rides on them (Psalm 18:10)

Two golden figures of cherubim sit above the Ark of the Covenant, where God promised to dwell among His people [34]

Cherubim are God's armed forces. Like God's version of the Marine Corp. No offense to the Marine Corp, but cherubim are much more powerful. If anyone is going to guard "Heaven's streets,"[35]

---

30 Colossians 1:16
31 Luke 24:39
32 Numbers 22:31, 2 Kings 6:17, Luke 2:13
33 Matthew 28:5; Hebrews 13:2
34 Exodus 25:22, see also verses 18–21
35 https://www.marineband.marines.mil/about/library-and-archives/

it will be Cherubim. Elite fighting forces like no other. Cherubs were placed outside the Garden of Eden to block the path to the Tree of Life from the rebelling angels and their emerging leader, Satan. Ibn Ezra says that the cherubs were "frightening images."[36] Rav Chaim Paltiel [37] suggests that the two statues of Cherubim on the Ark of the Covenant represent the two attributes of God, mercy and justice.[38]

When God dispatches His army to Eden, it represents justice. The fact that God does not forever eliminate the offenders in the Garden, represents His great mercy.

Cherubim represent "a kind of divine guard." This fits in with the description of the cherubs in Solomon's Temple as well,[39] which were ten cubits (twenty-two feet) high. Unlike the cherubs of the Ark, they were gigantic in size and instead of facing each other they both faced the door. The effect of such a display would be to intimidate people, forcing those who enter the room to be somber and frightening off unauthorized people who might be curious. Although this is true for Solomon's cherubs, the cherubs on the Ark, however, do not seem to be guards since they face each other not the outside, and are small and hardly intimidating.[40] The angels were not to be intimidating by themselves. Rather, it is not angels we should fear (or love), but the God who made them. Rabbinical literature makes it

---

the-marineshymn/
36   The Cherubim: Their Role on the Ark in the Holy of Holies. Dr. Rabbi Zev Farber
37   https://en.wikipedia.org/wiki/Chaim_Paltiel
38   Ibid. Farber.
39   1 Kings 6:23-28
40   Ibid. Farber.

very clear that angel worship is evil.[41]

"A number of biblical texts describe the cherubs as beings that haul God's chariot. This concept seems related to the idea of the divine chariot, which God is said to ride. Psalms 18:11 and 2 Samuel 22:11 describe God as riding a cherub,[16] but the most famous description of God riding a chariot is in Ezekiel. In truth, the term chariot does not actually appear in the chapters where the cherubs appear, but since God is described as riding the cherubs, with the cherubs apparently carrying God up into the sky,[42] it seems clear that they are carrying or functioning as God's chariot. Ezekiel describes God appearing to him while riding a divine chariot pulled by creatures with four faces and wings. Ezekiel calls these creatures cherubs.[43]

The Divine Throne

The Ark of the Covenant is often seen as a visible manifestation of the throne of God. Since God has no visible form, His interaction with mankind is usually done in some manifested presence. The Ark becomes a consistent method for this communication between God and the Children of Israel through the Levitical Priesthood.

- In a number of places in Tanach[44] we find that God is referred

---

41   Tosefta, Hollin 2:18; Gen. Rab. 3:8
42   Ezek. 10:15-20
43   Ibid. Farber.
44   1 Sam. 4:4, 2 Sam. 6:2, 2 Kings 19:15, Isa. 37:16

to as "the one who sits upon cherubs (מיבורכה בשוי)."

- God is said to dwell in the midst of the Tabernacle and speak from above the cherubs. Accordingly, many scholars understand the cherubs are likely part of the divine throne, a kind of platform upon which God will sit or stand and from which God will speak.[45]

It is evident that God, who is a spirit and thus has no image, chose to use the Mercy Seat as a visible throne. This was in fact the judgment seat of God. From here His grace and His mercy were equally distributed.

Cherubim is the plural version. Cherub is the singular version. For example, there were more than one sent to guard the Garden of Eden, so that is Cherubim. The cherubim are spiritual beings whose form is unknown. There are many ideas of what people think they look like, but these are just speculation. We do not know what God looks like and we do not know what these beings look like. Whatever they look like, we must be careful not to worship the wrong things. The artist renditions of what they speculate Cherubim looked like can lead to a form of angel worship. Angel worship is real. One form of angel worship is fashioned by those who worship Satan or Lucifer. We call this Luciferianism.[46]

---

45 William F. Albright, 'What were the Cherubim?', Biblical Archaeologist, 1 (1938): 1–3; Menachem Haran, Temples and Temple-Service in Ancient Israel (Oxford, 1978), 246–259. See Ezekiel 9:3, 10:1

46 gotquestions.org/Luciferianism.html

"You shall not make for yourself a carved image—any likeness of anything that is in Heaven above, or that is in the earth beneath ... "[47]

Ezekiel describes cherubim as bearers and movers of the divine throne. The cherubim do not turn as they change direction, but always go straight forward, as do the wheels of the cherubic chariot with rings full of eyes roundabout. The cherubim represent the spirit, or will, in the wheels: at the direction of the spirit, the wheels are lifted up from the bottom and the chariot moves upward. The cherubim are thus the moving force of the vehicle.[48]

The Prophet Ezekiel and Apostle John in Revelation speak of other kinds of Heavenly beings known as "living creatures" around God's throne. These are also Cherubim.[49] They appeared like a lion, an ox, a man, and an eagle, representing various parts of God's creation (wild beasts, domesticated animals, human beings, and birds). They, too, worship God continually: "Day and night they never cease to sing, 'Holy, holy, holy, is the Lord God Almighty, who was and is and is to come!'"[321] Some scholars see these four beings as representing the four gospels (Matthew, Mark, Luke and John).

Seraphim

Another type of angel, the seraphim, are only mentioned once in the Bible and may also be Cherubim. They appear in Isaiah 6:2–7, where they continually worship the Lord and say, *"Holy, holy, holy is*

---

47 Exodus 20:4
48 biblestudytools.com/dictionary/cherubim-1/
49 Ezekiel 1:5–14, Revelation 4:6–8 321 Revelation 4:8

the Lord of hosts; the whole earth is full of his glory." "The word Seraph means 'to burn.' When Isaiah saw the Heavenly realm, he witnessed some fantastic spiritual beings, but he could only use one word to describe them: Seraph — or "ones who burn."[50] Unlike God, who is omnipresent, angels are finite creatures, limited to one place at one time. The Bible does not tell us how many angels God created. Apparently, there are a lot of them.[51] Every biblical reference to the total number of angels suggests that they are beyond counting. Angels are definitely not to be worshiped. "Worship of angels" was one of the false doctrines being taught at Colossae.[52]

Today, angel worship is being taught by many churches, ministers, and denominations. In the book of Revelation, an angel warns John not to worship him: *"You must not do that! I am a fellow servant with you and your brethren who hold the testimony of Jesus."*[53] We should not pray to angels either. Only God is able to answer prayer. Paul warns us against thinking that any other "mediator" can come between us and God, "for there is one God, and there is one mediator between God and men, the man Christ Jesus."[54] If we were to pray to angels, it would implicitly give them a status equal to God. There are no examples in Scripture of anyone praying to an angel or asking angels for help. Moreover, Scripture gives us no warrant to seek appearances of angels. They manifest themselves unsought. To seek such appearances would seem to indicate an

---
50   Seraphim, Cherubim and Angels: Spirits of Fire. Lee Michael. Jul 28, 2019
51   Psalm 68:17, Hebrews 12:22, Revelation 5:11, Deuteronomy 33:2
52   Colossians 2:18
53   Revelation 19:10
54   1 Timothy 2:5

CHAPTER SIX: ANGELS

unhealthy curiosity or a desire for some kind of spectacular event rather than a love for God and devotion to him and his work. Though angels did appear to people at various times in Scripture, the people apparently never sought those appearances. Our role is rather to talk to the Lord, who is Himself the Commander of all angelic forces. However, it would not seem wrong to ask God to fulfill His promise in Psalm 91:11 to send angels to protect us in times of need.

Angels were already in existence before the Genesis account. We ascertain this because angels have nothing to do with the events of the creation story. In spite of what some theologians have offered, God needed no help with creation. There was no need for God to include information about whatever the angels were busy doing when He gave dictation to Moses to write Genesis. God's angels are faithful so it is not strange that they would be touring or roaming through His creation, granted access to the earth, and even the Garden of Eden.[55] They were quite aware of the activity here on Earth. Angels were the cheering section: "...and all the angels shouted for joy?"[56]

"Angels...were given many endowments from God. Pure spirits with a very keen mind and a strong free will. In the supernatural sphere they, like Adam and Eve, were given the state of grace, which is a sharing in the divine life and the divine nature."[57] *"An angel is a pure spirit, that is, an angel has no matter, no body. Each angel is a person (but not human), and has a mind and a will like ours, but angels are of a different kind (species) and from a different realm than*

---

55   Ezekiel 28:13
56   Job 38:4,7
57   The Fall of the Angels. January 3, 2014. John Flader

ours. They are sent by God for certain duties on this earth, in fact, the word angel means 'one who is sent' or 'messenger.'"[58]

"The Bible describes different varieties of angels. Angels are not former or future humans."[59] Angels are a different species (or kind). In fact, they are not remotely related to anything on earth because they are not of this realm. *"They are specially created beings that serve God and carry out His plans in Heaven and on Earth. God's Word tells us many things about them, but there is clearly much we do not know."*[60] It often seems like angels should be venerated. This is a carnal reaction because we see them as otherworldly. Part of this is true. Angels (all of them) are certainly not of this realm. Angels have their realm. Mankind has his realm.

Angels Are Soldiers, Not Supermodels

"Though impressive looking beings, angels should not be worshiped. The worship of angels was condemned by the Apostle Paul."[61] The angels are part of God's Heavenly Host. "Heavenly host" is a military term to describe a fighting unit. Ephesians 6 reminds us that we are in a war *"against the rulers, against the authorities, against the world powers of this darkness, against the spiritual forces of evil in the Heavens. Apparently, angels all have unique names, just like mankind. The first of only two angels mentioned by name in Scripture is Michael the archangel. He is God's chief warrior.*[62] Michael

---

58	Creation and the Angels. Rev. William G. Most
59	bibleref.com/Genesis/3/Genesis-3-24.html
60	bibleref.com/Genesis/3/Genesis-3-24.html
61	Ibid. Stewart.
62	Dan 10:13,12:1; Rev 12:7

is the equivalent of a five-star general or admiral."[63] Commander-in-Chief is a more appropriate title for Michael. Angels are powerful. One angel can do a lot of damage to the enemy. One angel killed 185,000 Assyrians in one day.[64]

What could an army of angels do? Only God knows. *"All of the Heavenly host, regardless of their classification, answer to their Commander in Chief; this is the Lord of Hosts! God is referred to as "Lord of Hosts,"* throughout Scripture[65] which is translated to "Jehovah-Sabaoth" or "Yhwh-Sabaoth" in Hebrew. "YHWH-Sabaoth" means "The Lord of Armies," which contemplates His righteousness and power over both spiritual and physical armies. According to MacLaren's Exposition, *"by that title, 'the Lord of hosts,' the prophets and psalmists meant to express the universal dominion of God over the whole universe in all its battalions and sections, which they conceived of as one ranked army, obedient to the voice of the great General and Ruler of them all."*[66]

Apostle Paul warns us, *"Do not let anyone disqualify you, insisting on self abasement and worship of angels, dwelling on visions, puffed up without cause by a human way of thinking."*[67] Apostle Paul's caution is a powerful point. The only one worthy of worship is the Lord of Hosts! It is evident that Apostle Paul is reminding those who follow Christ that we remain in a state of war. He warns against being beguiled by

---

63 Ephesians 6:12.
64 Isaiah 37:36
65 Haggai 2:4, Psalm 24:10
66 What Is the Heavenly Host? What Does Lord of Hosts Mean? Chad Napier
67 Colossians 2:18

enticing words.[68] This is reminiscent of the events in the Garden of Eden.

Apostle Paul is reminding us that it was listening to the words of an angel that started all of mankind's problems. Apostle Paul reinforces his admonishment with these words, *"Beware lest any man spoil you through philosophy and vain deceit, after the tradition of men, after the rudiments of the world, and not after Christ."*[69] Again, he is referencing the wild ideas that often result from the pursuit of carnality. He specifically mentions philosophy as a "love for wisdom."[70] his wisdom is the wisdom of the world. Remember the same writer said, "love not the world…"[71]

---

68 Colossians 2:4
69 Colossians 2:8
70 simple.wikipedia.org/wiki/Philosophy
71 I John 2:15-17

Chapter 7
Set your mouth to the trumpet

"In every DEED is a SEED! Everything about YOU matters. Every tear, trial & triumph is not just personal, but generational with rewards!"

– Pastor Phil Munsey

"Blow a trumpet in Zion; sound an alarm on my holy mountain! Let all the inhabitants of the land tremble, for the day of the Lord is coming; it is near, a day of darkness and gloom, a day of clouds and thick darkness! Like blackness there is spread upon the mountains a great and powerful people; their like has never been before, nor will be again after them through the years of all generations. Fire devours before them, and behind them a flame burns. The land is like the Garden of Eden before them, but behind them a desolate wilderness, and nothing escapes them. Their appearance is like the appearance of horses, and like war horses they run. As with the rumbling of chariots, they leap on the tops of the mountains, like the crackling of a flame of fire devouring the stubble, like a *powerful army drawn up for battle..."*[1]

War is a constant theme and backdrop in Scripture. We may not realize it at first blush, but if we pay attention to what is written we see a continuous theme set in military terms. Since war was declared by Satan and his angels, mankind has been at war. This is a no holds-barred winner takes all battle for the very souls of mankind. The impact of this war is a curse on the whole Earth. The Earth that experienced a period of peace during creation is shattered by war because of the deception by Satan and his angels. We generally say that God curses the earth. It is a minor point, but it rather seems that God is merely informing Adam and Eve of the results of their decision. A curse to be certain, but not brought by God's action. God is not bringing the curse. Satan brings the curse first to Adam and Eve. Then, the sin of Adam and Eve brings so much catastrophe through their posterity that the earth is maltreated. Satan used his status and position to betray God's trust. Satan commits the most subtle act of deception in history.

"Their actions aided Satan to defy the God of Creation."

In the same act, Satan betrayed the serpent that trusted his overtures held good intentions, to deceive Eve and liaised Adam. It is plausible that Satan may not have anticipated his plan would go so well that Adam would join the melee. It did not matter; the target was Eve, mother of all living. Satan had to corrupt Eve. She was the one he hated most. Corrupting her was satan's goal. His mission was accomplished. Adam

---

1   Joel 2:1-32 ESV

conscripted with Eve and by doing so gave his allegiance to Satan as a windfall. Little wonder God rails on Adam. Notice God does not say that Adam was deceived by the serpent. The fact of the matter is we have no evidence that Satan ever had a conversation with Adam. God said that Adam listened to his wife. Wow!

It is alarming, *"when you understand that these enemies of God's people have existed in other dimensions for thousands of years, and they are attempting to regain a foothold on society in these last days."* [2] It is likely that the penalties have not fully been considered by some of the parties. As is often the case when people commit crimes they focus more on the temporary benefits, the feel good, or the perceived reward. Adam and Eve traded not just life for death but immortality for death, Hell, and destruction! It is difficult for us to understand what it will be like to be immortal. Adam and Eve did not fully understand the impact of their decision to trade their immortality for death! Adam and Eve would have lived forever in the Garden of God. Instead, Adam and Eve became co-conspirators to Satan's War with God. Sadly, they became co-conspirators with a being that wanted their entire species eradicated! Stunning! They were not merely victims as it might be argued. Their actions aided Satan to defy the God of Creation. Their well-deserved punishment is banishment and much, much more.

We could get lost in useless diatribe about what kind of fruit was on the Tree of Knowledge of Good and Evil. We could debate, *"Was it an apple, a pineapple, a peanut?" "The Hebrew word 'peri' could be basically any fruit. According to Appelbaum, 'Rabbinic commentators variously*

---

2   Johnson. Chapter 3. Pg. 20.

characterized it as a fig, a pomegranate, a grape, an apricot, a citron, or even wheat. Some commentators even thought of the forbidden fruit as a kind of wine, intoxicating to drink.'"[3] "UGH!" Who really cares! The actions that result in betrayal, tumult and war are usually immaterial. Regardless of the justifications that might be presented, Adam and Eve were collaborators in a scheme by Satan to defy God, to defraud Adam, Eve and some earth creature. Scripture indicates that one-third of the angels were co-conspirators in this scheme.[4] The damage is eternal! The carnage is already immeasurable, and we are at the end. The victims will be innumerable.

Adam and Eve traded their amazing life, their daily communion with God for the empty words of God's new enemy. The creature that cooperated has much less to lose, but may also have traded eternal life for death. What about Satan? Well, our adversary, the devil called Satan, traded an exalted place in the Kingdom of Heaven for the life of a fugitive and ultimately eternal damnation.[5] Satan may not have fully grasped the penalty for his treachery. The price of disobedience to God is heavy. It is probable that Cain echoed the thought of all the betrayers, "my punishment is more than I can bear."[6] Yet, even this is a deception. God who is Righteous and merciful never places more on us than we can bear,[7] and the penalty for Cain's sin is more than reasonable. If he had received justice, he would have been put to death. Fortunately for Cain, he was a

---

3   Did You Know ... The Fruit of the Tree of Knowledge was NOT an Apple? Scott Smith. MARCH 12, 2018. Page 1.

4   See Revelation chapter 12

5   Matthew 25:41

6   Genesis 4:13

7   I Corinthians 10:13

recipient of God's mercy. Sadly, for mankind, Cain and his posterity were as bad (if not worse) for mankind as were Adam and Eve.

In response to the horrible deeds of Satan in the Garden of Eden, God dispatches His armed forces. The presence of the sword-bearing Cherubim stresses that Adam and Eve were forcefully expelled from the Garden of Eden. The word cherubim is plural, indicating several angelic beings...who completely blocked the way to the Tree of Life. The added facts that the sword was flaming and "turned every way" (indicates that each angel had a sword) also emphasize the strong security God had provided.[8] This presents that this army of angels had swords drawn prepared for battle. There was no possibility that Adam and Eve or any other being could later reach the Tree of Life. What had previously been the source of eternal life was now unreachable.

This action is obviously not just about Adam and Eve. Respectfully, God did not need an angel army to hold back two mortals. Adam and Eve presented little threat to the security detail at Eden. God could have set a couple of rottweilers to keep Adam and Eve out of Eden. The military response reveals a threat much larger than the two mortals who gave up their immortality. The challenge that has come is bigger than just a war on mankind. War had come to the whole earth and it could be presented that war has come to the entire Universe. Satan has enlisted a large portion of the angelic host to assist him in his ignoble cause. War has replaced peace on Earth! The goal does not present as them believing they can be God. Rather

---

8 https://www.gotquestions.org/guard-east-Eden.html

it presents like a family feud. Some of the angels are not willing to be subservient to mankind.

> *"Now the Lord God had planted a garden in the east, in Eden...The Lord God made all kinds of trees grow out of the ground — trees that were pleasing to the eye and good for food. In the middle of the garden were the tree of life and the tree of the knowledge of good and evil."*[9] "God not only planted this garden, He refers to it in a very personal way.[10] In multiple places, God's Word refers to the Garden of Eden as "the Garden of God" or "the Garden of the Lord."[11] It is evident that this is a very special place in the eyes of God. *"Brings entirely different imagery to mind. We're not saying God wore a floppy straw hat or had dirt under his nails. We're just saying that the picture the Bible paints is of God's very hands-on involvement in planting a garden He calls His very own. This Garden was, indeed, a very special place."* God has prepared this garden as a special place to nurture the man and the woman. We often refer to it as paradise. It is that and much more.[12]

The man and the woman that God put in Eden got the attention of the angelic host in general and obviously Satan. Ironically, later in Genesis we find a story where Jacob gives considerable attention to one son while seemingly giving less to the other sons. The Scriptures tell us that Jacob loved Joseph more than any of the other brothers. This favoritism to Joseph caused

---

9   Genesis 2:8, 9

10   7 Interesting Things You May Not Have Considered About the Garden of Eden. Karen Scalf Bouchard May 30, 2019.

11   Isaiah 51:3

12   Ibid. Bouchard.

his brothers to hate him.[13] This favoritism is only the beginning of the story. Later the story erupts into a very personal war between Joseph and his brothers that lasts for decades. Like his father Jacob, Joseph is a dreamer. One of his dreams indicates that he will be placed in a position where his brothers and perhaps even his parents will do obeisance to him. This is too much for the brothers. Their envy, jealousy, and hatred reach a boiling point only waiting for opportunity. Like Cain who killed his brother, the brothers decide they will kill their brother Joseph.[14] Fortunately for Joseph, the brothers do not kill him. They decide instead to sell him into slavery.

The similarities between this story of Joseph and the story of Adam and Eve are simply unmistakable. It is no stretch to understand that the angels likely felt some level of jealousy or envy toward Adam and Eve who resided in such a special place. A place God planted. A place where God Himself walked with Adam in the cool of the day.[15] Seriously? Which one of the angels do we ever find at any time that God walked with them? Well, none! There is no such account. It is evident that this was a daily event for Adam and God. This intimacy certainly did not go unnoticed. It certainly does not go unnoticed by another "special creation." The Prophet Ezekiel gives us this picture:

"...I ordained and anointed you as the mighty angelic guardian. You had access to the holy mountain of God and walked among the stones of fire. "You were blameless in all you did from the day you were created..."

---

13   Genesis Chapter 37
14   Genesis 37:18-20
15   Genesis 3:8

WAR ON EARTH

It is apparent that while God is quite delighted with His creation,[16] the favored status of Adam and Eve is the source of great discontent in the hearts of Satan and a sizable faction of the angels. What is the source of this discontent? Some scholars see the source of this discontent as causing a War in Heaven. We are given little insight to such a notion as a war in Heaven until the book of Revelation is written. If there is a war in Heaven as these scholars claim, then when did the war start? More importantly why? They claim that *"Sometime before the events of Genesis chapter 3 and likely after Genesis Chapter 1 there was a War in Heaven with Satan and one-third of the Heavenly host choosing to side against God in some Heavenly version of mutiny or Civil War."*

We know that there was great harmony in Heaven. It appears that Heaven, previous to this time was… well, Heavenly! The angels were happy. God was so pleased He was focusing on His new "sandbox" project He was calling Earth. God created a bunch of different creatures for His Earth project! Everything was good! God continued to improve His Earth project with some notable additions. God made a man. Whatever a man was, and even that was good! Visualize the angel's conversation about all of this:

Angel 1: *"Have you seen what God is working on?"*

Angel 2: *"Yes. I saw He made a new creature the other day. He calls it a man."*

Angel 1: *"What does he do?"*

---

[16]   Genesis 1:31

CHAPTER SEVEN: SET YOUR MOUTH TO THE TRUMPET

Angel 2: *"Well, he is like a zookeeper and gardener all rolled into one."*

Adam certainly was the zookeeper and gardener. God gave the man the job of overseeing His Garden. The angels apparently looked on in wonder.[17] One thing was not good, the man was all alone.[18] Don't worry, God fixed that as well. He created a woman for the man. Everything seems quite perfect. So, why does Satan show up in Paradise masquerading as some creature and trying to mess things up? Suppose you are building sandcastles on a beach. Just as you have the perfect one — here comes a wave. The sandcastle is wiped out! What brought about this sudden turn of events in the Garden? Or was it sudden? How long had God's new creation been around we cannot be certain. We do know that Adam could have not been more than 100 years old when Eve was created. So, it seems that if some part of creation, or Adam was the challenge, it would have manifested sooner. There was a newcomer. The newcomer was the woman. Could the creation of the Woman have anything to do with the change in the thoughts and actions of some of the angels including the one we refer to as Satan?

Most Bible scholars postulate that there was a war in Heaven between chapters 1 and 3 of Genesis. This concept has become popular largely because of John Milton's well-known work of fiction, "Paradise Lost."[19] It is strange but not uncommon for a book of fiction to be given such status, but there are many who give such preference even over the Word of God. Our mission in this writing

---

17 I Peter 1:12
18 Genesis 2:18
19 https://en.wikipedia.org/wiki/Paradise_Lost

is not to create a work of fiction but to find the real answers. There is no reference in the book of Genesis of a war in Heaven. The theologians that offer this idea wrest the Scriptures saying that the story of a war in Heaven had to be before Genesis Chapter 3.

Oddly, God dictated these important details for Moses to record for all mankind. Theologians want us to believe God forgot to give Moses such an important detail. It seems obvious that God would not have neglected such an important detail as a war in Heaven, if there was such an event. The fact of the matter is there is no reference of a war in Heaven until the book of Revelation.

Let us focus on what we know. Satan was a welcomed visitor to the Garden of Eden. This was "the Garden of God"[20] a showcase of God's creation! His special interest in Adam and Eve is like a proud Papa talking about his children.[21] These were God's children. The future was bright for the sons of God. With their elevation, the pecking order seems to change for angels. Apostle Paul speaks to this point, "But to which of the angels has He ever said: *"Sit at My right hand, Till I make Your enemies Your footstool?"*[22] *"Everyone who believes that Jesus is the Christ has been born of God, and everyone who loves the Father loves whoever has been born of Him. By this we know that we love the children of God, when we love God and obey His commandments. For this is the love of God, that we keep His commandments. And his commandments are not burdensome. For everyone who has been born of God overcomes the world. And this is the victory that has overcome the world — our faith. Who is it that*

---

20   Ezekiel 18:12-13
21   Psalm 127:3
22   Hebrews 1:13

CHAPTER SEVEN: SET YOUR MOUTH TO THE TRUMPET

overcomes the world except the one who believes that Jesus is the Son of God?"[23] The prophecy of Genesis chapter 3 is fulfilled. This son of Adam and Eve is now ruler of all creation!

Evidently, the combination of the future destination of mankind and the sort of demotion for angel kind was just too much for Satan and a plethora of his angelic friends. Here they decide to draw the proverbial "line in the sand." They are not going to stand by and watch "their rightful place" be pre-empted by mankind. Of particular concern is the woman. Unlike any of the angels, Adam was created with the ability to produce offspring. The angels could only imagine such a thing. When Adam was created, it did not really matter, but when the woman was created that was a game changer. The woman was the perfect match for Adam and the ability to procreate made her a unique source of life. Obviously, some of the angels and their apparent leader Satan pondered the remedy and an evil plot was born.

If the woman was somehow out of the picture, then things could get back to normal. It is sadistic to infer that God sent Satan to deceive Eve. God loves His creation.[24] Adam and Eve were His special children. Eve's deception and Adam's willingness to join the charade were painful! Had Satan not hidden his deception God would have never allowed him in the Garden of Eden. As soon as God sees Satan's deed, God dispatches His army![25] Satan used the trust God gave him to take advantage of God's creation. Satan knew

---

23 I John 5:1-13
24 See John 3:16
25 Genesis 3:24

the exact layout of the Garden and the living arrangements of the first couple. He would have known details such as the creatures they trusted, interacted with, used for pets and more. He not only violated the trust of God, Satan violated the trust of Adam and Eve. This was happening. The Rebellion of the ages had begun! Satan was going to go to war with Almighty God! This was not War in Heaven — that would be too bold. This was war on Earth! War in Heaven will come much later!

Satan was not going to walk into the throne room, shake his fist at God, and explain his superiority! No, this was far more subtle. Satan would deceive the woman; she would take the bait because he was extremely crafty. God would see how useless, unworthy, and unappreciated Adam and Eve were of His attention. Satan's angel friends apparently embraced the plan. The sooner they were rid of the woman the better. Satan's angels would not sit idly by and let these neophytes usurp their proper place with God. This war on Earth is the beginning of many things. The angelic host is divided. Now, there are Satan's angels and God's angels. The classic battle of Good vs Evil has begun. For Satan, he is kind of like God's pet dog and he mauled somebody horribly.

When mankind begins to rationalize, or philosophy error is often the result. In Genesis 3, the philosophy of the serpent convinced Eve that rebelling against God in favor of Satan would be permissible. *"Genesis gives us the first mention of a cherubim in Scripture. Cherubim angels are mentioned over 90 times in the Old Testament. Ezekiel 1 and 10 describe them as powerful winged creatures. They almost always serve*

CHAPTER SEVEN: SET YOUR MOUTH TO THE TRUMPET

in the capacity of guarding or protecting what belongs to God or even His own presence."[26] The cherubim in Genesis are assigned to guard the way to the Tree of Life. If you expect that God dispatches His "special forces" to secure the area around His garden in response to Adam and Eve, you have missed the point. This is no simple action to keep a few (Adam, Eve and eventually their children) rebellious people out of a garden. The response is not overkill. God is not using a machine gun to kill a mosquito. Quite the contrary, God has dispatched His army for a specific reason. The reason is a real threat! That threat could be recognized as Satan and his angels.

We must consider if it would take an army of cherubs (cherubim) to defeat Satan. It does not seem likely. What is more likely and even glaringly obvious is the cherubim are dispatched as part of a military strategy to keep Satan and his horde of angels from getting to the Tree of Life. The Bible mentions the tree of life again, when it shows up in the new Heaven with the Lord.

Revelation 22:1-3 notes, *"Then the angel showed me the river of the water of life, bright as crystal, flowing from the throne of God and of the Lamb through the middle of the street of the city; also, on either side of the river, the tree of life with its twelve kinds of fruit, yielding its fruit each month. The leaves of the tree were for the healing of the nations. No longer will there be anything accursed." "The closing chapters of the Bible describe a restored Eden, complete with the Tree of Life and the river that flows from His throne. The whole narrative of Scripture finds its fulfilment when the King announces the restoration of the Edenic ideal:"*[27]

---

26   GOD'S ANGEL ARMY. Mark Dance. December 22, 2014
27   Ibid. Browne

> *"And I heard a loud voice from the throne saying, "Look! God's dwelling place is now among the people, and he will dwell with them."*[28]

> *"Eden, the Tree of Life, and the river that sustains life — these are all symbols of the sovereignty of the realm. He rules from Heaven, yet He lives among his people on earth, providing a garden associated with his presence, and sustaining life throughout his realm."*[29] *"What a picture: King YHWH, living among his creatures, providing for them, and honoring humans with participation in his reign! Can you imagine what life on earth would be like if it had always remained like this? This is the hors d'oeuvres of the kingdom: does it pique your appetite for the banquet?"*[30]

---

28   Rev 21:3 (NIV)
29   Ibid Browne.
30   Ibid. Browne.

Chapter 8
Satan is defeated

"Adam surrendered the eternal to live in the temporal. Jesus surrendered the temporal to live in the eternal"

– Brian S. Wade

One of the challenges for those of us who are mortal is to comprehend that the goal must be to put on immortality. This mortal will put on immortality…[1] Jesus said, "He came to save that which was lost."[2] Notice He did not say that He came to save those who were lost, but that which was lost. What was lost? Eve lost her immortality when she followed the words of Satan. Jesus Christ came to restore a path for us to immortality!

---
1   I Corinthians 15:53-55
2   Luke 19:10

Then the seventh angel sounded: And there were loud voices in Heaven, saying, *"The kingdoms of this world have become the kingdoms of our Lord and of His Christ, and He shall reign forever and ever!"*

Counterfeit Kingdom

Satan is a mimic. Mimicry is probably his best skill set. Everything that he does mimics the genuine. "The first recorded incident of identity theft is reported in Genesis, chapter 3. Satan used the serpent to trick Adam and Eve into believing that God had selfish motives for not allowing them to eat from the Tree of Knowledge of Good and Evil. Like modern day con artists and hackers, Satan's actions were motivated by discontent, jealousy, and envy. His tactics were based in lies, pretense, and deception. His goal was simple — to destroy the confidence that Adam and Eve had in their identity as children of the Most High God. He used trickery and deception to attack their personal identity and relationship with God by causing them to doubt God's love for them, to question His Word and will for their lives, and their rights and privileges as children of God — to have dominion and power over all the earth with unlimited access to God. They believed Satan's lies more than God's promises, they disobeyed God and ate from the Tree of Knowledge of Good and Evil. In this one act of disobedience the fate of mankind was changed forever."[3]

"You are my hiding place and my shield; I hope in Your word."[4]

---

3   hbu.edu/center-for-christianity-in-business/2015/04/06/identity-theft-beganin-the-garden-of-eden/

4   Psalm 119:114

CHAPTER EIGHT: SATAN IS DEFEATED

While the curse is rightly named, God is a God of judgment (justice) and mercy. In His proclamation, God points out the punishment for sin, but also points to a day of redemption for all of the seed of the woman. *"The curse on the serpent[5] sets the stage for the subsequent course of redemptive history.[6] From the book of Genesis, the theme of 'enmity between offspring/seed' characterizes the biblical narrative. This is ultimately fulfilled in Jesus Christ, the consummate 'seed of the woman' who crushes the head of the serpent. In the three curse-speeches given in Genesis 3:14–19, the plotline of history is sketched out."*[7]

It is never God's intention to leave mankind in a hopeless situation. Rather, the intent is for mankind to come to the realization that our only hope is in Him. The late Billy Graham said this: *"For the believer there is hope beyond the grave, because Jesus Christ has opened the door to Heaven for us by His death and resurrection."*[8] *"It's said that those who don't know history are doomed to repeat it. I believe this is a true statement. People are people. Human nature is human nature. People in the present will make similar mistakes others made before them, mistakes that could be avoided if they had studied history. The divinely inspired Word of God gives us history — true history, beginning with the creation of the world. In the beginning, God created the Heavens and the Earth — the universe and everything in it. The Lord created human beings, made in His image, male and female, and placed them in a delightful garden in the Middle East and warned them not to eat the fruit*

---

5 Genesis 3:14–15
6 Luke 10:19; Romans 16:20; and Revelation 12:17
7 The Seed of the Woman. R. Andrew Compton
8 https://billygrahamlibrary.org/5-verses-on-hope-found-in-jesus-christ/
382 https://www.shema.com/before-the-beginning-what-happened-before-genesis-1-8792/

of the Tree of the Knowledge of Good and Evil. The woman was tempted by the satanic Adversary and disobeyed the Word of God by eating from the Tree of the Knowledge of Good and Evil. The man joined her."[382] The choices were simple. Eat of the Tree of Life equals Eternal Life. The other Tree equals Death. We can only imagine the shame, disgrace, and sadness that fell on Adam and Eve as they were evicted from their home in the Garden of God. Their attempts to blame others for their moral failure were fruitless. Even more difficult to comprehend is how God must have felt. One of His created beings concocted a most egregious plan and then acted on the plan. The plan was for the genocide of all mankind; Mankind, God's special creation. The only creation made in His image. His special children had succumbed to the evil conspiracy. Satan knew full well that the ruse he pulled to dupe Adam and Eve brought the death penalty. He lied about the penalty of death in his effort to deceive God's children. Envy drove Satan to want the destruction of mankind more than anything. Satan understood God's word is even more unalterable than the law of the Medes and the Persians (A law that altereth not).[9] In order to achieve his malevolent plan Satan had to convince Eve to violate the one law of God that held the death penalty.[10] This was no accident. For whatever reason(s) it is evident that Satan remains immortal despite his planning the scheme that set man up to fall from immortality. Although, he will pay an eternal penalty.

God had already spoken on the subject. Adam and Eve were instructed that violating God's law would mean death. Still, the God

---

9   word histories. MEANING AND ORIGIN OF 'THE LAW OF THE MEDES AND PERSIANS'. Pascal Tréguer

10   Genesis 2:17.

of creation formulated a plan to redeem fallen man. Nevertheless, man who was immortal dealt with the ravages of sin for millenniums until the coming of Jesus Christ. Those who rather than call upon the name of the Lord,[11] choose to follow Satan's direction and reap horrible consequences. The sons of God,[12] those elect that God created to serve Him, even these acquiesce to the lure of the world. The penalty is death. God loves His children. There remains a penalty to sin, but in spite of their horrible decisions, God has a strategy for redemption. God's covenant with mankind is in force even though man has not upheld His end of the agreement.

God brought swift and sudden death to nearly all the posterity of Adam and Eve. Strangely, there is no record that either Adam or Eve ever repented. Yet, God extended the covenant He made with Adam and Eve on to Noah, his wife, and family. They carried on the mandate God had given Adam and Eve. In a love that surpasses our understanding God continued His plan for mankind.[13] *"Even the holy angels are struck with astonishment at the plan of human redemption, and justly wonder at the incarnation of that infinite object of their adoration. If then these things be objects of deep consideration to the angels of God, how much more so should they be to us."*[14]

Satan and his co-conspiring angels began their war on mankind in the Garden of Eden. They pilfered the rightfully held

---

11 See Genesis chapter 4
12 See Genesis chapter 6
13 Psalm 8:4
14 Adam Clarke Commentary. 1 Peter 1:12

dominion that God gave to mankind. Satan set up his strategic position in this stolen territory. To bolster his claims, he makes many self-promoting assertions about his control of mankind and the earth. Since that time both mankind and Earth have remained in a constant state of war. There have been a plethora of conflicts, skirmishes, and battles. The warfare is intense, with periods of nearly total destruction of mankind.[15] Adam and Eve's son Cain kills his own brother. When God confronts Cain about his sin, he is not willing to repent.

Instead, like Isaiah's references of Satan, Cain moves as far away as he can from the presence of God and establishes a lineage of people that continue rebellion against God. His most notable descendant is Enoch. This Enoch's identity is synonymous with those who defy God.[16]

Adam and Eve's other son, Seth, leads a different life and his descendants attempt to find their way back to relationship with God. These are some of the many of those referred to as sons of God. Among the most famous of his descendants is also Enoch. This Enoch is one of those sons of God that walks with God.[17]

Even these sons of God eventually become corrupted by Satan's venom, God opts for the nuclear option and destroys the inhabitants of the whole earth in the Great Flood. Noah, his family and a select group of animals are the only survivors. Estimates of

---

15 Genesis chapter 7
16 Genesis 4:17, 18
17 Genesis 5:18, 21–24; Jude 14, 15

the death toll range from millions to billions.[18] The message is very clear. God has low tolerance for those who repeatedly disobey and teach others to follow in their footsteps. Despite the expectation of better things, the descendants of Noah mostly failed as miserably as their ancestors. There were bright spots along the way. One of Noah's descendants, Abraham would carry the vision and burden of God's redemptive plan all the way to Jesus Christ. Jesus Christ would pay the redemptive price for all mankind by shedding His sinless blood on Mount Calvary. Rightly does Isaiah prophesy of the coming Messiah.[19]

In the long list of attributes that would be fulfilled by Jesus Christ, Isaiah calls Him "El Gibbor" the prevailing or conquering God.[20] There are many instances of the conquering God in the Scriptures. The Prophet Elijah is involved in one of these. *"Elijah was not afraid of the forces amassed against them, for he saw the reality in the spirit realm. They were surrounded by a great army that looked like it was on fire, for the angelic armies of God carry his fiery, purifying, light-giving presence."*[21] Satan's angels understood the power of this conquering God. When Jesus Christ interacts with a man possessed by devils, they try to intimidate Him with their numbers.[22] They say, "We are many." No matter Jesus casts them all out. He holds all power

---

18   https://biblescienceguy.wordpress.com/2014/06/18/4-population-growth-how-manydied-in-noahs-flood/

19   Isaiah 9:6-7

20   Adam Clarke. Isaiah 9:6

21   Seraphim, Cherubim and Angels: Spirits of Fire. Lee Michael. Jul 28, 2019

22   Mark chapter 5

WAR ON EARTH

in Heaven and Earth...[23] On Mount Calvary, God contracted once and for all with mankind's transgressions. Christ becomes the only being in history to raise Himself from the dead![24] Christ conquers death, Hell, and the grave! Satan is defeated! As often is the case, mankind is looking into the Heavens for answers that are much closer to home.[400] It is our expectation that the events of Genesis triggered war on Earth. Satan's willingness to become the first recorded sinner establishes him as the leader of the faction of angels that orchestrate this attack on mankind. That action simultaneously erupted in a war with God and all that is called Holy. That war decimated mankind in ways unimaginable. Mercifully, at Calvary things forever change.

Satan lays claim to the title, god of this world.[25] Like other titles of Satan, god of this world is not a compliment. It is a title of the one who leads the children of disobedience[26] as opposed to the sons of God. It indicates being potentate of only those who God is going to destroy. *"One way to understand this title 'god of this world' is to realize Satan's rule is limited. He has the ability to oversee evil in our world, but lacks the power to defeat God and rule in Heaven."*[27] Rex, the king of Mardi Gras holds more authority.[28] It is kind of like being made god of Winterfest. As soon as winter is over, your kingdom melts! Satan and the demons, sin and the sin nature, and death took control

---

23   Matthew 28:19
24   I Corinthians 15:20
25   2 Corinthians 4:4
26   Colossians 3:6
27   compellingtruth.org/satan-god-world.html
28   https://en.wikipedia.org/wiki/Rex_parade

of mankind *in Genesis chapter 3. Demons are some form of manifestation of satan's angels. "The Old Testament is remarkably reticent about evil spirits. There are no incantations, rituals or amulets prescribed for giving an individual protection from spirits. Considering how much of the Torah is devoted to ritual and to sacred objects, this is a remarkable omission. God is said to have complete authority over the spirits, which cannot operate in the world without his approval. If a 'lying spirit' goes out, it is only with divine consent.[29] The main concern of the Old Testament writers was that people avoid seeking to avail themselves of magical powers through contact with spirits.[30] The New Testament demonstrates two realities about evil spirits: Jesus alone has absolute power over them, but this is a matter of divine authority, not magic or sorcery.[31] The New Testament mocks the claims of magicians by describing their inability to deal with real spirits. Simon the sorcerer [32] and the sons of Sceva (Acts 19:14–16). Jesus had no use for demonic spirits and did not seek to employ them to do His bidding."[33]*

It likely seemed to Satan and his angels that they had won. Adam and Eve's death would give them superiority to mankind. Their assumptions were very wrong. The Lord (gracious, merciful, and compassionate) provided temporary atonement for Adam and Eve by means of the death of innocent animals. Along with that temporary atonement, He promised them perfect, ultimate, eternal atonement. From the Seed of the Woman, a son would be born who would defeat the Adversary and undo all the damage that the Evil One had caused but in the process of bringing redemption, the Seed

---

29 1 Kings 22:23; cf. Job 1–2
30 Deuteronomy 18:10–12
31 Luke 4:41
32 Acts 8:9–24
33 olivetree.com/blog/demons-in-the-bible/

of the Woman would be wounded — a reference to Messiah's death.[34]

We know that the early generations advanced technologically, but worsened morally and spiritually — much like today. We know that things got so bad that the Lord destroyed that first civilization with a worldwide flood, but spared Noah and his family, whose descendants began to repopulate the earth. We know that there was a rebellion against God at the tower of Babel, and God divided humanity into various nations with different languages. We know that God created a special nation that would be a light to the other nations and be the nation through which the Seed of the Woman would come.[35] Theologians have offered that the war in Heaven began before Genesis 3. There is no Scripture to substantiate these theories. We have uncovered that the beginning of this war in Heaven is war on Earth. This began in Genesis chapter 3.

War in Heaven

What exactly is happening in chapter 12 of Revelation? In Genesis we discover that Adam and Eve have willfully sinned and surrendered their immortality.[36] Satan has stolen the dominion mankind has over the earth. In effect, Satan has stolen man's blessing. Just like a big bully. Like taking candy from a baby, Satan took the things God had given His children and he is not about to give them back without a fight. After millennia of warfare, God

---

[34] https://www.shema.com/before-the-beginning-what-happened-before-genesis-1-8792

[35] shema.com/before-the-beginning-what-happened-before-genesis-1-8792/

[36] Hebrews 10:26

CHAPTER EIGHT: SATAN IS DEFEATED

comes to get back what was stolen from His children. God is not tolerant of deception. In Scripture, Jacob uses deception to get his brother's birthright. For a while it seems he will get by without consequence. Not so fast! God does not let this stand and confronts Jacob.

In this life changing event God changed Jacob's name from supplanter to Israel — A prince with power through God.[37] Someone who has a name celebrating human aggression is not going to be the progenitor of God's special children. So, the name change is necessary. Only God can grant blessings.[38]

Satan is not bashful about what he has pilfered. He offers the rewards to those who serve him. He even offers the same to Christ Jesus.[39] Imagine offering stolen property back to the father of the children it was stolen from in exchange for being your subject! In the interaction between Satan and Jesus Christ, Satan does not comprehend with whom he is negotiating. Unlike Eve, Jesus Christ prevails over the offers of the Tempter.[40] As usual, Satan's underlings do not take no for an answer. They remain busy putting their plot into motion. The goal is the same as in Genesis. Murder mankind! Exterminate the seed of the woman. For Satan and his angels, it seems that their work against mankind is coming to fruition. Even the one they call King of the Jews is facing death.[41] Satan does not

---

37 https://en.wikipedia.org/wiki/Israel_(name)#:~:text=Word%2F-name-,Hebrew,Related%20names
38 Genesis 32:22-32
39 Matthew 4:1-11
40 Luke 4:1-13
41 Luke 23:3

realize that his time is running out! God is about to confront Satan about his crimes.

The Woman, the Child, and the Dragon by the time of the New Testament, it had been a long time since the first prophecy of the coming Messiah.[42] At last He has come. Jesus Christ is the long-promised Messiah. Even the angels are in agreement that Peace has finally come to the war-torn earth. The Prince of Peace has come, but there is still much to be done. A battle rages. The war that was enjoined in Genesis 3 is coming to another critical juncture. Apostle John sees it this way,

> *"Now a great sign appeared in Heaven: a woman clothed with the sun, with the moon under her feet, and on her head a garland of twelve stars. Then being with child, she cried out in labor and in pain to give birth. And another sign appeared in Heaven: behold, a great, fiery red dragon having seven heads and ten horns, and seven diadems on his heads. His tail drew a third of the stars of Heaven and threw them to the earth. And the dragon stood before the woman who was ready to give birth, to devour her Child as soon as it was born. She bore a male Child who was to rule all nations with a rod of iron. And her Child was caught up to God and His throne."*[43]

As pledged so long before, the Seed of the Woman has finally come to the battle. Apostle John gives us an amazing vision received from God. In this vision Satan saw the woman give birth through great pain as promised in Genesis 3. At this historic intersection some

---

42   Genesis 3:15
43   Revelation 12:1-6

CHAPTER EIGHT: SATAN IS DEFEATED

seventy-six generations of women have endured pain in childbirth. [44] To be certain we recognize who Apostle John's vision of the woman represents, we are reminded that she is clothed with sun and moon. Thus, she represents the lineage of the sons of God as promised to Abraham, Isaac, and Jacob. The son and the moon represent both the man and the woman (Adam and Eve). Just like in Joseph's dream where he speaks of the sun and moon and Jacob rightfully discerns this is him and his wife.[45] This daughter of Eve gives birth to the promised man-child who represents both the 12 tribes of Israel and the 12 Apostles. As usual, Satan shows up even though he is not invited. He is represented as a great red dragon. In like manner as the Prophets Isaiah and Ezekiel, Apostle John describes Satan in language that also could be applied to Satan's cronies. In Apostle John's vision they represent the Roman Emperor and Empire.

Apostle John explains that the war began on Earth is reaching into the Heavenlies.

"The Pagan empire, as under the influence of Satan, the god of this world, is fitly compared to a 'dragon,' for its policy and cunning in circumventing and ensnaring those who profess Christ; and for its cruelty and inhumanity in persecuting of them; and for its poison of idolatry, worship, and superstition: and it may be called a 'great' one, for its strength and power, which lay in its immense treasure and riches, in numbers of men, in powerful armies, in strong cities, castle and for its large extent and jurisdiction; and a 'red' one, because of the blood of the saints shed in it, by which it became of this color; suitable to the character and bloody practices of the old serpent the devil, by whom it was influenced, who was a

---

44   Luke chapter 3
45   Genesis 37

murderer from the beginning."[46]

Revelation chapter 12 emerges as a vision of the events surrounding the crucifixion of Jesus Christ and the unseen battle in the spirit realm. Apostle John is given insight into the spirit realm as to the things that happened "behind the scenes." Apostle John, though present at the crucifixion of Jesus Christ and surrounding events, had no foresight into this spirit realm. Jesus Christ through Divine Revelation unveils to the Apostle those things that have already happened as well as things that were happening and would happen in the future.[47]

The Woman Gives Birth to a Child

We are given a plethora of clues to his identity. It is a male child to whom has been given ruler ship (dominion). Dominion is one of the things Satan coveted and usurped in the Genesis confrontation with mankind. The only being ever granted dominion by God is Adam.[48] A child that Satan tried to devour as soon as it was born. This is true both in the spirit realm and in the natural. Adam and Eve are devoured by Satan. Satan seeks to devour all their children especially Jesus Christ.[49]

This speaks to the imprimatur of human empires as well as

46	John Gill's Exposition of the Whole Bible. Revelation 12
47	Revelation 1:19
48	Genesis 1:26
49	1 Corinthians 15:45

CHAPTER EIGHT: SATAN IS DEFEATED

Satan's malevolent schemes and aligns with similar passages in Isaiah and Ezekiel. God easily sees Satan's influence and speaks directly to the situation. Herod, a surrogate, uses the imprimatur of the Roman empire in his attempt to kill the Christ child. This is prophesied and confirmed in Christ Jesus.[50] *"In Genesis, Rachel dies giving birth while on the road to Bethlehem. In the midst of her suffering, the midwife tries to comfort her with the news that she is having another son. In this way, her child is both her cause of weeping and her hope for the future. In Jeremiah's day, Rachel weeps over her children once more, this time because they are being led into captivity and exile near the very spot where she is buried. She is then comforted with the promise that her children will return. Once again, her offspring are both her cause of weeping and her hope for the future. In Matthew's day, Rachel weeps yet again: this time over the slaughter of the children at Bethlehem. The situation seems bleak, but the hope of salvation lives on."*[51] The history of Satan's plan to annihilate the children of God is horrifying.

"When the wicked king Herod orders the slaughter of innocent children to protect his rule, we naturally think of the Egyptian pharaoh who ordered the slaughter of Hebrew children. One child, Moses, escaped the slaughter and went on to deliver his people from captivity and exile. In the same way, Jesus escapes the slaughter of the innocents — ironically, by going into exile in Egypt. Like the Israelites, he is led into Egypt by a man named Joseph, a man whom God speaks to in dreams. Like the Jews for whom Rachel wept in Jeremiah's day, this child knows the experience of living in exile, and like the Israelites of Moses' day, he goes through his own exodus from Egypt. Just as Rachel was comforted with the promise that her children would be restored, and just as Moses' birth was a sign

---

50   Jeremiah 31:15 and Matthew 2
51   Why is Rachel Weeping at Ramah? Part 3. DECEMBER 19, 2012. DAVID LANG

that the Israelites' deliverance was near, so the long-awaited Messiah has been born salvation is close at hand."[52]

More important that the natural attributes of the woman are the Spiritual ones. Apostle John is writing to the sons of God. It is important they understand to whom they belong. This woman represents the Church. The Bride of Christ, purchased with His own blood. The target of Satan since Genesis was not just the woman, (Eve) but the Seed of the Woman which would manifest first in Christ and then with His blood bought bride. The sons of this woman would change the whole earth and lead those who desired to be righteous to become the sons of God. While there are literal explanations that show this gendering to the Roman Empire, the horns and the heads represent the kings of the earth and their allegiance to Satan. Seven representing completeness and ten representing government or authority. The kingdoms of this world have all given their authority to Satan. Sadly, for them, their self-exalted leader is exposed for the fraud that he has always been. The battle for mankind is full force. All of these have given their power to the beast, a creature representing Satan.

The rod of iron prophesied by the psalmist has come in the person of Messiah.[53] Apostle John is well aware the Messiah has come in Jesus Christ. A king that holds all power and authority has come. *"The manner which Christ will rule, especially over His enemies, whom He will destroy with the breath of His mouth, and break in pieces with His rod of iron, and order all that would not have him to reign over them slain before Him;*

---

52 Ibid. Lang
53 Psalm 2:9

and as this may be applied to Christ mystical, the seed of the church, and members of Christ. The strongholds of Satan were pulled down, not by carnal, but spiritual weapons; when multitudes of souls were converted by the word, the rod of Christ's strength, and when the saints were guided, directed, fed, and comforted by it; for the allusion seems to be to the shepherd's rod, with which he leads and feeds his sheep; the same word signifies both to rule and feed." [54]

Satan Loses Access to Heaven

"And war broke out in Heaven: Michael and his angels fought with the dragon; and the dragon and his angels fought, but they did not prevail, nor was a place found for them in Heaven any longer. So the great dragon was cast out, that serpent of old, called the devil and Satan, who deceives the whole world; he was cast to the earth, and his angels were cast out with him." [55]

The war on Earth that began in the beginning for mankind, now is engaged in the Heavens. Michael is named here. Michael, the theophany of Jesus Christ, representing the Commander-in-Chief of God's armed forces, engages in a battle for the ages with the adversary of all mankind. Satan's free reign has come to an end. The battle for mankind is raging while Jesus Christ hangs on a cross at Mount Calvary and lies in the tomb. Satan expected this to be his greatest triumph. Satan who has deceived the whole world will lose this battle. Satan and his angels expect they will win a decisive battle against another Son of Eve in like manner they have repeatedly accomplished throughout the history of mankind. Although, this Son of Man has

---

54 John Gill's Exposition of the Whole Bible. Revelation 12
55 Revelation 12:7-9

proven to be more difficult than any of the rest. Satan used his best deceptive techniques and Jesus Christ did not fall for any of them. The victory by Jesus Christ is more decisive than Satan realized. One of the curses of this battle is that Satan and his angel co-conspirators lose access to Heaven. This entire fulfillment of prophecy by the psalmist:

> *"The chariots of God are tens of thousands and thousands of thousands; the Lord has come from Sinai into his sanctuary. When you ascended on high, you took many captives; you received gifts from people, even from the rebellious — that you, Lord God, might dwell there."*[56]

Apostle John is not the only Apostle to see Jesus as a conquering King! Apostle Paul gives us similar insight into the victory. The whole of this verse, just as in Psalms, refers to military triumph. Adam Clarke commented this: *"Thou hast ascended on high: the conqueror was placed in a very elevated chariot. Thou hast led captivity captive: the conquered kings and generals were usually bound behind the chariot of the conqueror, to grace the triumph. Thou hast received gifts for (Paul, given gifts unto) men: at such times the conqueror was wont to throw money among the crowd. Even to the rebellious: those who had fought against him now submit unto him and share his munificence; for it is the property of a hero to be generous. That the Lord God might dwell among them: the conqueror being now come to fix his abode in the conquered provinces and subdue the people to his laws."*[57]

"All this the apostle applies to the resurrection, ascension, and glory of Christ. Thou hast received gifts for men,[58] thou hast taken gifts in man, in

---

56   Psalms 68:17-18
57   Adam Clarke Ephesians Chapter 4
58   lakachta mattanoth baadam

CHAPTER EIGHT: SATAN IS DEFEATED

Adam. The gifts which Jesus Christ distributes to man He has received in man, in and by virtue of His incarnation; and it is in consequence of His being made man that it may be said, The Lord God dwells among them; for Jesus was called Immanuel, God with us, in consequence of His incarnation. This view of the subject is consistent with the whole economy of grace, and suits well with the apostle's application of the words of the psalmist in this place."

War began in the Garden of Eden. War enslaved all of mankind. This war has come to a decisive battle. Satan is cast down to the earth by the Conquering King! Jesus Christ is exalted as King of all the other kings! Satan's best was not nearly enough to defeat the true King of Glory! Satan is he *"who opposeth and exalteth himself above all that is called God, or that is worshipped; so that he as God sitteth in the temple of God, shewing himself that he is God."*[59] He has lost access to Heaven. Satan, accuser of the brethren, is cast down to the earth leaving only one Champion. Only one ascended being. The one who came down from Heaven and also ascended back into Heaven is Triumphant![60]

"Then I heard a loud voice saying in Heaven, "Now salvation, and strength, and the kingdom of our God, and the power of His Christ have come, for the accuser of our brethren, who accused them before our God day and night, has been cast down. [11] And they overcame him by the blood of the Lamb and by the word of their testimony, and they did not love their lives to the death.[12] Therefore rejoice, O Heavens, and you who dwell in them! Woe to the inhabitants of the earth and the sea! For the devil has come down to you, having great wrath, because he knows that he has a short time."

---

59   2 Thessalonians 2:4
60   Acts 1:11

The key to Revelation chapter 12 comes with "Now Salvation..." All of creation has been waiting for the coming of Messiah and His Triumph! He alone can bring salvation to mankind.[61] He alone holds the strength! His Kingdom is announced! SATAN IS DEFEATED! Jesus Christ has all the power![62]

"The kingdoms of this world have become the kingdoms of our Lord and of His Christ, and He shall reign forever and ever!"

The Heavens are told to rejoice! Why? It's because they no longer need to worry about Satan and his angels. They have lost access! The war in Heaven has been decided. Jesus Christ is the Victor! On the other hand, the inhabitants of the earth are warned that Satan, now groveling in the dust of the earth is very angry! Of course, he is angry! This usurper has been dealt with just as promised in Genesis chapter 3! The seed of the woman has bruised his head!

The Woman Persecuted

Since the moment Satan and his angels conceived the idea to deceive Eve, mankind has been at war. The war comes to a crucial juncture when Jesus Christ comes to set things right.

"Now when the dragon saw that he had been cast to the earth, he persecuted the woman who gave birth to the male Child. But the woman was given two wings of a great eagle, that she might fly into the wilderness to her place, where she is

---
61   John 14:6
62   Matthew 28:18

nourished for a time and times and half a time, from the presence of the serpent. So the serpent spewed water out of his mouth like a flood after the woman, that he might cause her to be carried away by the flood. [16]But the earth helped the woman, and the earth opened its mouth and swallowed up the flood which the dragon had spewed out of his mouth. And the dragon was enraged with the woman, and he went to make war with the rest of her offspring, who keep the commandments of God and have the testimony of Jesus Christ."[63]

As always, the battle is about the true sons of God. Satan is at war with them. He makes war with the offspring (seed of the woman) of the people of God. Those sons of God who are in covenant with Jesus Christ. The ultimate target that Satan sought in the Garden of Eden. The target that first caused him to assault Eve is now in full display. The curse that Satan would find his abode in the dust of the earth has come to execution. Through the seed of the woman has come forth the one that brings salvation. In the Garden of Eden Satan enacted a master plan to seize the authority given to mankind. Dominion of the earth would be his. Satan would accomplish his ultimate goal. He and his angels would not be subservient to mankind. His goal to have mankind be subservient to him worked very well from Adam to Noah. Then, God eliminated all of Satan's followers with the Great Flood.

"It was Jesus Himself who, in the Spirit, preached 'to those who were disobedient long ago when God waited patiently in the days of Noah while the ark was being built. We take this to mean that, when Noah preached righteousness, he did so by the power of the Spirit of Christ: that is, it was the message of

---

63   Revelation 12:13-17

Christ, delivered in the power of Christ, that Noah proclaimed. The ungodly men of Noah's day had a chance to repent and be saved as Christ preached to them spiritually through Noah. Unfortunately, they rebelled against the truth, refused the ark, and drowned in the flood."[64] There Satan lost his slaves. God did what seemed impossible. He killed all of his man creatures except eight. In some measure it must have seemed to Satan that he was winning his chess match with God. All of mankind destroyed certainly met his goals. Only eight to go! What Satan does not see is God's redemptive plan being deployed. The flood was only the beginning. In the economy of God, who is timeless, being delayed does not mean denied. While God concedes the bulk of mankind as lost due to their allegiance to Satan, he also gives mankind hope for a brighter tomorrow. Noah, the first preacher of grace ushers in a new lease on life for mankind.[65] For God, the end game is always the same in His plan for the redemption of mankind.

What Satan stole from mankind in the beginning, Jesus Christ restored. What looked like defeat in the Garden of Gethsemane was the culmination of more than 75 generations of the plan of God for the redemption of mankind. Satan was defeated from the moment he betrayed God by the deception of His children in the Garden of Eden. The journey for mankind from the Garden in Eden to the Garden in Jerusalem held many defeats and triumphs for mankind. The coming victory over death, Hell, and the grave would usher in a glorious new age. Jesus Christ reigns as the long-awaited legitimate King of all mankind.

---

64   1 Peter 3:19–20
65   2 Peter 2:5

CHAPTER EIGHT: SATAN IS DEFEATED

What Was Satan's Sin?

Satan conspired with other angels to attempt the genocide of all mankind. Their target was Eve. Eve had been created immortal in the image of God Himself. She was given dominion (ruler ship) and the ability to reproduce. Unlike the angels which have no bodies, Eve was the only created being that could produce other immortal beings. Envy of Eve drove Satan and his angel allies to their sin in the Garden of Eden. This act against Adam and Eve, who were God's special children, triggered war between mankind and angel kind. This war raged with horrible consequences that ended with the destruction of all but eight of mankind. Satan immediately went to war with the eight survivors of the Great flood. From Noah to Jesus Christ is a long history of mankind and his triumphs and defeats in the battle between Good (God) and Evil (Satan and his angels).

When did Satan commit this sin that theologians present as causing his (and his angel co-conspirators) expulsion from the Heavens? God repeatedly presents that everything is very good through the first two chapters of Genesis, the war had to begin in Genesis 3 or later. There is no war on Earth in the first two chapters of Genesis. God makes certain that Moses writes that everything is fantastic (very good)![66]

---

66   Genesis 1:31

Why Did Satan Deceive Eve? Was He Angry? Insane?

Satan was driven by his envy of Eve. She was his target. He became drunk with coveting that she had been given dominion and the ability to make man in covenant with God. God granted her this right by covenant with Adam and by connotation Eve. Eve is the progenitor of mankind. God made the first man and then equipped man's helper with exactly what she needed to fulfill the covenant and make other men in God's image.

"And God said, Let us make man in our image, after our likeness: and let them have dominion over the fish of the sea, and over the fowl of the air, and over the cattle, and over all the earth, and over every creeping thing that creepeth upon the earth." [67]

Why Did Satan Not Attempt To Deceive Adam?

We have no indication that Satan even spoke to Adam. This presents Adam as irrelevant to the conversation that led to the deception. It may be argued that Adam was not included because he may have stopped Eve from disobeying God. However, the Scripture presents that Adam sinned after listening to his wife — not the serpent. However, Eve obviously repeated the words of Satan to Adam. Adam was not chastised because he listened to the woman, he was chastised because he listened to Eve instead of the command God had given him. Both parties are equally valuable, they may have

---

[67] Genesis 1:26-27

different roles in His plan but each wouldn't be able to achieve that without the other. Satan targeted Eve because of her unique role in God's plan for mankind.

Why Did God Allow Satan To Cause Chaos In Eden?

Satan is a created being. Satan is angel kind. As such, like mankind, God gave him free will. His pride drove him to see the destruction of mankind because mankind was created higher than the angels and Satan and his angels were not willing to be subservient to mankind.[68]

Why did God not just pre-empt Satan's antics? God did not stop Satan because Satan was permitted to choose. The direction that Satan chose was a horrible choice. However, people make horrible choices every day. Could God stop them? Yes, theoretically, but He will not because He has allowed them to choose.

Did God Purposely Allow Satan To Tempt Eve As Some Teach?

God cannot sin.[69] Satan in collaboration with or at the urging of some of God's angels concocted a plan they expected would lift them above mankind in God's economy. They postulated that the death of mankind would seal mankind's fate. They did not expect that God would have a redemption plan for fallen man.

---

68   Hebrews 1:4-14
69   1 John 3:9

Why Did Adam Join In Satan's Deception?

Like most sin, Adam does not seem to give much thought to the consequences. Adam and Eve failed to keep the Commandments of God. This led to all of their posterity being born cursed (born in sin and shaped in iniquity). [70] Satan promised to make them like God, but NEVER delivered. Jesus Christ came to restore what was lost by Adam and Eve and give all mankind the opportunity to choose eternal life.

> *"And I give them eternal life, and they shall never perish; neither shall anyone snatch them out of My hand. My Father, who has given them to Me, is greater than all; and no one is able to snatch them out of My Father's hand. I and My Father are one."* [71]

---

70 John 8:21-24
71 John 10:28-30

CHAPTER EIGHT: SATAN IS DEFEATED

WAR ON EARTH

www.ingramcontent.com/pod-product-compliance
Lightning Source LLC
Chambersburg PA
CBHW072016110526
44592CB00012B/1325